Narrative Toolbox

Blueprints for Storybuilding

Peg Hutson-Nechkash, M.S., CCC–SLP

Thinking Publications • Eau Claire, Wisconsin

09   08   07   06   05   9   8   7   6   5   4   3

Library of Congress Cataloging-in-Publication Data

   Hutson Nechkash, Peg, date.

      Narrative toolbox : blueprints for storybuilding / Peg Hutson Nechkash.

        p. cm.

      Includes bibliographical references.

      ISBN 1-888222-61-1 (pbk.)

      1. Storytelling. 2. Discourse analysis, Narrative. 3. Children's stories—Study and teaching (Elementary). I. Title.

      LB1042.H86 2000

      372.67'7—dc21   00-050941

Printed in the United States of America

Cover Design and Illustrations by Kris Gausman

THINKING
PUBLICATIONS®
A Division of McKinley Companies, Inc.

424 Galloway Street · Eau Claire, WI 54703
715.832.2488 · Fax 715.832.9082
Email: custserv@ThinkingPublications.com

COMMUNICATION SOLUTIONS THAT CHANGE LIVES®

To my parents,
Tom and Betty Hutson

Contents

Preface vii

Part 1: Introduction 1

    Overview 3

    Rationale 3

    Goals 4

    Target Users 4

    Background 4

        Narrative Skill Development 4

        Story Grammar 8

        Narrative Skill Difficulties 11

        Developing Children's Narrative Skills 13

        Assessing Narrative Skills 14

    Using *Narrative Toolbox* 16

        Presenting the Lessons 16

        Transitioning to Written Narratives 19

        Monitoring Progress 19

    Final Thoughts 19

Part 2: Lessons 21

    Introduction to Story Grammar Elements 23

        Story Grammar Octopus 25

        Story Train 30

    Story Setting 35

        Character Descriptions 37

        Character Changes 42

        Character Comparison 46

        Additional Character Activities 49

        Place Comparison 50

        Creating a Mood 53

        Setting the Stage 59

        Additional Place Activities 62

        Time Machines 63

        Time Chance 67

        Additional Time Activities 70

Contents

Story Problem 71

    Introduction to the Story Problem 73

    First Event Categories 76

    First Event Scripts 81

    Response Card Game 86

    Stating the Goal 96

    Making a Plan 101

    Seeing the Attempt 106

Story Solution 111

    Outcome and Ending 113

Solving the Story Puzzle 117

    Retelling a Complete Episode 119

    Using Story Glue 126

    Introducing a Story 133

    Retelling a Story with a Complex Episode 137

    Stories with Multiple Episodes 144

    Using Embedded Episodes 151

Written Narratives 159

    Writing a Note 161

    Writing a Story 167

    Taking Messages 170

Appendices 175

    Appendix A: Narrative Levels Analysis Form 177

    Appendix B: Retelling Rubrics 178

    Appendix C: Story Creation Rubrics 180

    Appendix D: Story Rating Scale 182

    Appendix E: Recommended Children's Literature 183

    Appendix F: Strategies for Reading Stories Aloud 186

    Appendix G: Scaffolding Questions 187

    Appendix H: Story Maps 190

    Appendix I: Feedback Form 192

    Appendix J: Story Scenes 193

References 197

Preface

Since the 1990 publication of *Storybuilding: A Guide to Structuring Oral Narratives,* the importance of narrative development has become increasingly evident. Narrative assessment is now standard practice in the evaluation of a student's communication skills. But after one identifies students with deficiencies in their narrative skills, he or she needs a structured approach to expose children to story grammar skills. *Narrative Toolbox* was written to meet this need.

I would like to thank my editors at Thinking Publications—Linda Schreiber and Angie Sterling-Orth—for their guidance, encouragement, and insights. I would also like to express my appreciation to the reviewers—Sarah Bennett, Kris Wisniewski, and Holly Witt—whose contributions broadened and strengthened this book. A special thank-you to Shannon Mauger for her exciting illustrations that were used during the prototype stages of this project.

Over the years, I have spoken to many other speech-language pathologists at conferences, conventions, and classes. Thanks to all of you for your feedback about *Storybuilding. Narrative Toolbox* is a better resource because of those comments.

A final thank-you to John, Tim, and Sam.

Introduction
Part 1

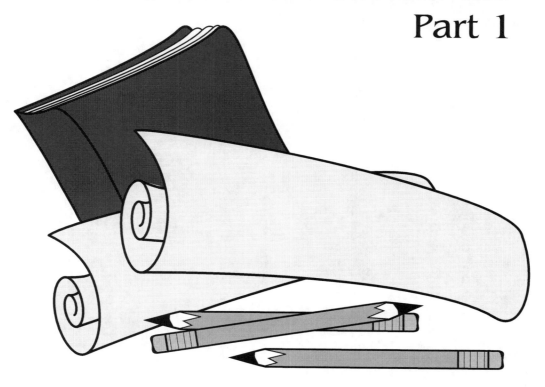

Overview

Narrative Toolbox is a resource for speech-language pathologists, special education teachers, general education teachers, and teachers of English as a foreign language. In an organized, sequential way, *Narrative Toolbox* exposes students in grades 3–8 to the story grammar elements (adapted from Stein and Glenn, 1979) of a complete narrative: setting (character, place, and time), first event, response, goal, plan, attempt, outcome, and ending. Through the activities in this resource, students have multiple opportunities to practice identifying individual story grammar elements and to learn how to combine these elements to form complete narratives, namely, fictional stories.

Narrative Toolbox is divided into two parts. Part 1 provides an introduction to the resource, including such areas as goals; background information pertaining to narratives; narrative development and story grammar elements; and procedural information for using the resource. Part 2 includes dozens of activity lessons to help students better understand and use the story grammar elements. Within each lesson, all procedural information and any necessary reproducible pages are provided.

Following Part 2, a wealth of useful forms and other handy reproducible pages are provided in the Appendices. Parts 1 and 2 explain when and how to use these pages.

Rationale

Narratives can be found throughout a student's entire day. In a social studies class, a student might be asked to create a narrative highlighting key dates in history. In a science class, a student might need to explain the steps of an experiment. While waiting for the school bus, a student might tell another student about the movie he or she watched the night before. During supper, a child might be asked to tell about the events of his or her school day. Academically and socially, narratives play an important role in communication. "Children's skill at producing oral narratives allows them to gossip, express peer solidarity, impress, clarify, inform, tell jokes and anecdotes, empathize, criticize, persuade, threaten and befriend" (Crais and Lorch, 1994, p. 14).

At school, at home, and at all grade levels, students may be asked to construct oral narratives to describe, to explain, and to interpret events. In addition to producing narratives, students are expected to be adept at comprehending information presented in narratives. A student's inability to form or comprehend narratives may be incorrectly interpreted as a lack of knowledge or understanding. Clearly, students with limited narrative skills are at a disadvantage in social or academic settings. *Narrative Toolbox* is a resource to help such students discover the blueprints for building narratives.

Goals

The goals of *Narrative Toolbox* are the following:

- Increase students' knowledge of story grammar elements to facilitate narrative comprehension
- Provide students with opportunities to develop story grammar skills and practice telling stories
- Help students practice and generalize use of oral and written narratives for academic and social purposes

Target Users

Narrative Toolbox is intended for use with students in grades 3 through 8. Many of the activities require that students possess at least a minimal level of reading and writing skills. However, modifications can be made for students who are nonreaders. The activities in this book are ideal for students with language and learning disabilities; they are equally useful for students who need to develop story grammar skills. The activities work best for small-group instruction, but they can also be used with individual students and large groups.

Background

The term *narrative* refers to an "orderly continuous account of an event or series of events" (Nicolosi, Harryman, and Kresheck, 1996, p. 177). In a narrative, the speaker (or writer) presents extended text using a specific internal structure that helps the listener (or reader) understand the story and form idea expectations. The listener's (or reader's) role is passive, so the speaker (or writer) is expected to be clear, organized, and interesting (Roth and Spekman, 1986).

As a search of the literature demonstrates, there are a many ways to describe and categorize narratives. Hedberg and Westby (1993) refer to five common types of narratives: scripts, recounts, accounts, event casts, and fictional stories. Descriptions of each of these narrative types are presented in Table 1.

Skilled communicators are proficient at utilizing many types of narratives. The activities in *Narrative Toolbox* focus on fictional stories since the skills required to produce these types of narratives can also be applied to other narrative types. According to Hedberg and Westby (1993), "People who are able to comprehend and produce fictional stories will most likely be able to comprehend and produce other types of narratives as well" (p. 2). In addition, fictional stories are familiar to children and are present in all societies and cultures.

Narrative Skill Development

Children's understanding and use of narratives is an integral component of language development. Among a child's first narrations are the stories he or she tells when looking at picture books or

Table 1	Types of Narratives

Scripts

Expressing knowledge of a familiar, recurring event. Usually told using the second person pronoun *you* and the present tense.

Recounts

Telling about a personal experience when prompted. Usually told using the past tense.

Accounts

Telling about a personal experience without a prompt. The experience is usually not shared by the listener.

Event Casts

Explaining an ongoing activity, reporting on a factual scene, or telling about a future plan.

Fictional Stories

Relating past, present, or future events that are not real. The events being described focus on someone or something attempting to carry out a goal.

Source: Hedberg and Westby (1993)

retelling favorite stories. During the primary school years, narrations are evidenced in show-and-tell and sharing time. A child's understanding and use of narratives also plays a role in connecting home and school experiences. During the middle and high school years, a student's personal narratives may serve as the basis for writing tasks, speeches, and other assignments. Children who have difficulty structuring narratives can encounter significant trouble throughout their school years (Scott, 1988).

When asked to make up a story, children will sometimes begin the narrative with "Once upon a time…" indicating that this more literary style has been incorporated into their repertoire. Children learn this literary style through repeated exposure to books and stories. "Listening to and reading high-quality literature allows students to experience all the language components together and promotes narrative development" (Van Dongen and Westby, 1986, p. 80).

Children acquire narrative skills not only through exposure to well-formed stories, but also by practicing these skills. Children as young as two or three years of age will relate stories to listeners (Kemper and Edwards, 1986). Van Dongen and Westby (1986) state, "Children's development of narrative discourse grows within the context of their daily lives, as they tell personal narratives about themselves and others and build their experiences and knowledge about the world" (p. 71).

The acquisition of narrative skills follows a developmental progression, with early developing skills providing the foundation for later acquired skills. Applebee (1978) outlined six early stages in the development of narrative skills that parallel stages of concept development set forth by Vygotsky (1962). Applebee's stages apply to fictional narratives (stories) and personal stories (accounts), but not to scripts. These six stages are described in Table 2 on pages 6–7.

Narrative Toolbox

Table 2

Applebee's (1978) Narrative Stages

	Approx. Age of Emergence	Description	Example
Heaps	2 years	*Heaps* are collections of unrelated ideas, which are actually considered prenarratives. Children switch topics freely with no apparent connections between utterances. The sentences are generally simple declarations, usually in the present or present progressive tenses (Westby, 1984). Cohesive techniques are not used. "Children who tell heap stories often do not appear to recognize that the characters on each page of picture books are the same characters" (Westby, 1984, p. 115).	A dog is walking down the street. A cat is fighting the dog and a baby is crying. The baby is sleeping. The boy is playing on the swing. The man is laying down and the girl is jumping the jump rope. The lady is cooking chocolate chip cookies. A girl is going to the store. The man is going into the supermarket. The old man is fighting the other man. That's all. (Hedberg and Stoel-Gammon, 1986, p. 62)
Sequences	2–3 years	*Sequences* represent the second stage of prenarrative development. The term *sequences* is confusing since the elements of the stories are linked together by arbitrary commonalities but without a common characteristic. Sequences do include a macrostructure, which involves a central character, topic, or setting. "The story elements are related to the central macrostructure on perceptual bonds" (Westby, 1984, p. 115).	She lives with her dad. She lives with her mother. Grandma and Grandpa live together. And these three children live with their grandma. And these two animals live with them. And that's all. (Hedberg and Stoel-Gammon, 1986, p. 62)
Primitive Narratives	3–4 years	*Primitive narratives* typify the next level of narrative development. Like the sequence stories, primitive narratives contain a macrostructure of a central character, topic, or setting. Unlike sequences, the events in a primitive narrative follow from the central core. This main theme requires the child to interpret or predict events. "Children producing primitive narratives recognize and label facial expressions and body postures, and in their stories they make frequent reference to the associated feelings of the character" (Westby, 1984, p. 117). Children at this level of narrative development do not always recognize the reciprocal causality between thoughts and events (Larson and McKinley, 1987). Cohesive techniques, such as pronominals (e.g., *this, any, some*) and reiteration of the main character's name may be used. These techniques link individual sentences to the major theme but not to each other.	My dad, he went up to go to work. My mom stayed and slept in. My two brothers, they went to go play with the toys. My dog, she went outside. My kitty cat came up and he tickled me and came up and started to meow. And then I started to cry because he bit me. And my brothers came runnin' in and Mike said, "What happened?" They said, "What happened?" "My kitty cat just bit me." So mom comes runnin' in and she said, "What happened? Oh, the kitty cat bit you. O.K." (Hedberg and Stoel-Gammon, 1986, p. 62)

Table 2—Continued

	Approx. Age of Emergence	Description	Example
Unfocused Chains	4–4½ years	*Unfocused chains* contain no central character or topic. These chains present an actual sequence of events, yet there is no consistency of character or theme. The events are linked in logical or cause-effect relationships. Cohesive techniques of connecting words (e.g., *well*) and propositions (i.e., the referent of the sentence) may appear. The conjunctions *and*, *but*, and *because* may also be used. This type of narrative structure is seldom produced by children for as soon as cause-effect and sequential relationships appear, children begin to tie the story elements to each other and to a central theme (Westby, 1984).	*This man is walking. He saw a dog and a cat and he saw a girl, too, with the cat and the dog. He said, "Hello." "He walked back and he said, "Brother, come here." So her grandmother walked up to her and said, "You wanna go dancing?" They went dancing. And so it was a slow dance. And then they went back. And then these two children came. And then first he said, "I'm not." And then he said, "What?" "I wanna go out to eat." So they went out to eat. (Hedberg and Stoel-Gammon, 1986, p. 62)*
Focused Chains	5 years	*Focused chains* are composed of a central character and a logical sequence of events. These stories describe a chain of events that take the form of a series of "adventures." Even though there are central characters and a true sequence, the listener is left to interpret the ending. Westby (1984) states, "the characters' actions seldom lead to attainment of a goal; consequently, if no goal is perceived, then, in the child's thinking, there is no need for an end to the story, or, at least, the ending does not have to follow logically from the beginning" (p. 118).	*Once upon a time there was a mother named Christie. And she had a husband named Tom. And they had some children named Heather and Christie. And then they had a boy named Ronnie. And the mother told the boy to go outside to play. And then the boy came in and said, "Mother, mother, our dog's outside and he's barking." "I will go see." "What are you barking at?" "I don't know what he was barking at, Tommy, Ronnie, Ronnie. I don't know what he was barking at. You go out there and see." "He wants in." "I'll go let him in." "There, I let him in." (Hedberg and Stoel-Gammon, 1986, p. 62)*
True Narratives	6–7 years	*True narratives* represent the next stage of narrative development. True narratives adopt a consistent perspective focused on an incident in a story. There is a true plot, character development, and a true sequence of events. The presented problem, which is related to issues introduced in the beginning, is resolved in the end. Children may also perceive and relate the relationship between attributes of characters and events. Children continue to lengthen and refine their narratives after they have developed the use of true narratives. The specific elements of a narrative also grow more complex as children mature (Applebee, 1978).	*One day there was a boy named Bobby and a girl named Sharon. They found a cat in their front yard and they brought it into the house. They fed the cat and they gave it some milk. They played and played with it and then a little while after a lady called and asked if anybody had seen her cat. And then they said that they had it at their house. And they brought it to the lady's house. And she gave them each five dollars for finding the cat and having them feed it and give it milk. (Hedberg and Stoel-Gammon, 1986, p. 62)*

Sources: Applebee (1978); Hedberg and Stoel-Gammon (1986); Westby (1984)

Narrative Toolbox

Applebee also suggests four higher level stages of narrative development, based on Piaget's levels of cognitive development (Ault, 1977). These stages are as follows:

Narrative Summaries (7–11 years)

At this level of development, children begin to summarize and categorize stories. Children may categorize stories subjectively or objectively. "Subjectively, the child may categorize or summarize a story as 'funny' or 'exciting' or 'sad.' Objectively, the child may summarize a story as rhyming or long. In either case, the child is capable of considering the entire story and placing it in a more general category" (Larson and McKinley, 1987, p. 100).

Complex Narratives (11–12 years)

Children at this level of development are capable of producing complex stories with multiple embedded narrative structures.

Analysis (13–15 years)

Adolescents who reach this level of development are adept at analyzing stories. This analysis is often combined with the evaluation of stories or of specific elements of stories.

Generalization (16$^+$ years)

Individuals at this level of narrative development are capable of more sophisticated analysis. When presented with a story, these individuals are now able to generalize about the story's meaning, formulate abstract statements about the message or theme of the story, and focus on their reaction to the story (Larson and McKinley, 1987).

Story Grammar

Story grammar refers to the organization of a narrative based on causal and temporal relationships (Hughes, McGillivray, and Schmidek, 1997). Story grammar includes typical elements found in most fictional stories, specifically setting and episode details. The use of story grammar seems to represent the speaker's knowledge of narrative structure and the degree to which the speaker allows the listener to assimilate the narrative input (Roth and Spekman, 1986).

Narrative abilities start with *story schema,* which is a mental representation of the structure of a story (Hughes et al., 1997). As knowledge of story schema develops, a child acquires expectations of the types of information in a story and the relationships that link the story elements. Development of story schema helps a child encode as well as decode information in a story.

Children as young as age 5 are aware of the organization of basic stories and use this organization as the framework for the comprehension of stories they hear and for the creation of original stories (Stein and Glenn, 1979). While several different story grammar models have been proposed (see Nelson, 1993, for a review), the model most often used in the analysis of children's fictional narratives is that developed by Stein and Glenn.

Stein and Glenn (1979) assert that a story is composed of a setting and one or more episodes. Episodes can be complete or incomplete. According to Stein and Glenn, a complete episode must contain a minimum of these three elements:

1. An initiating event or an internal response

2. An attempt

3. A direct consequence

Narrative Toolbox uses a modified version of Stein and Glenn's (1979) model for outlining story grammar elements. The model has been modified to make it more explicit for students. Specifically, students learn three main parts of a story: the setting, the problem, and the solution. The term *initiating event* was changed to *first event,* the term *reaction* was changed to *response,* and the terms *goal* and *plan* were added. Finally, the *consequence, resolution,* and *ending* elements delineated by Stein and Glenn were changed to the more simple elements of *outcome* and *ending.* Table 3 differentiates Stein and Glenn's model from the story grammar framework used in *Narrative Toolbox.*

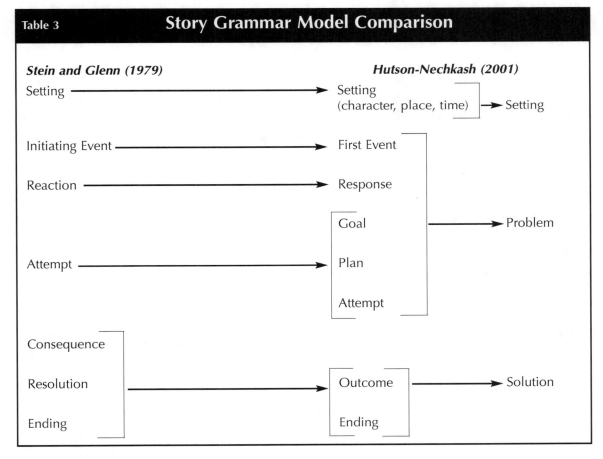

Table 3 — Story Grammar Model Comparison

Stein and Glenn (1979)	Hutson-Nechkash (2001)	
Setting	Setting (character, place, time)	Setting
Initiating Event	First Event	
Reaction	Response	
	Goal	Problem
	Plan	
Attempt	Attempt	
Consequence		
Resolution	Outcome	Solution
Ending	Ending	

The following is a description of each story grammar element, adapted from Stein and Glenn (1979) and targeted in *Narrative Toolbox.*

Narrative Toolbox

Setting

This component begins the story and allows the rest of the story to happen. The setting tells where and when the story takes place and who the characters are. In a simple story, the setting occurs first; in a longer, more complex story, this information may occur when there are changes in time or location and when there is an addition of a new character.

First Event

Known as the initiating event in Stein and Glenn's (1979) model, the first event is the situation to which the character must respond. It may be a natural occurrence, such as a weather change; an action, such as something a character does that affects another character; or an internal event, which is a change in the character's state.

Response

The response is the state of the character following the first event. In other words, how the character feels or what the character is thinking in regard to the first event.

Goal

What the character hopes to achieve or attain is the goal.

Plan

The plan is the character's strategy for attaining the goal. In stories that have just a few events, the plan may not be clearly stated but may be inferred from the events. The plan is most apparent when the character recognizes that there will be obstacles to reaching the goal and establishes subgoals that will lead to reaching the ultimate goal.

Attempt

What the character does to reach the goal is the attempt.

Outcome

The character's success or failure in reaching the goal is the outcome. It is often directly related to the first event.

Ending

The ending is a statement indicating the conclusion of the story. The ending may also summarize the story or state a lesson learned.

This story grammar model does not perfectly characterize all stories. Rather, it provides a framework for viewing children's stories and helping students acquire story knowledge. Both narrative structure and story grammar elements should be considered when assessing and targeting narrative skills. Story grammar and narrative assessment allow us to evaluate and make judgments regarding a student's ability to structure and produce an oral narrative.

Story grammar skills develop throughout childhood and, in turn, affect the complexity of a child's narratives. Preschool- and elementary-aged children might not tell narratives that contain all story grammar elements. However, a fictional story produced by an adolescent should contain all story grammar elements (Larson and McKinley, 1995). Glenn and Stein (1980) have suggested a developmental taxonomy for the pattern of story grammar development. Eight different levels are identified, ranging from the least to the most complex. Each level contains all the components of the previous levels with one additional component added. A description of each level is presented in Table 4 on page 12.

Narrative Skill Difficulties

Many students with language-based learning disabilities struggle with narrative skills. These students may:

- Produce stories typical of children much younger than themselves (Silliman and Wilkinson, 1991)

- Take a considerable amount of time to construct a story (Silliman and Wilkinson, 1991)

- Demonstrate difficulty understanding and generalizing new information for the purposes of telling a story (Silliman and Wilkinson, 1991)

- Lack the awareness of pragmatic and emotional elements required to comprehend and tell a story (Coleman, 1997)

In a study comparing spontaneously produced stories told by students with learning disabilities to stories produced by their peers without learning disabilities, Roth and Spekman (1985) reported that the stories told by students with learning disabilities were shorter, contained fewer descriptors, had less detail, and included substantially fewer complete episodes. Furthermore, students with learning disabilities demonstrated less usage of response, plan, and attempt statements and were less likely to connect related statements, as compared to their peers.

Students with language-based learning disabilities also struggle with reading and writing skills. Therefore, these students do not receive a sufficient amount of practice reading and writing well-formed stories with complete story grammar elements. Without this important exposure, these students end up in a vicious circle, without the needed opportunities to develop their narrative skills. Oral narrative skills, reading skills, and writing skills are interrelated, effecting and stimulating one another. Norris and Brunig (1988) examined the narratives of 150 skilled and struggling readers in kindergarten and first grade. Their findings indicate that struggling readers produce stories that are shorter, contain fewer ideas, and include more irrelevant information. In addition, struggling readers seem less likely to tie story grammar elements together and to link characters and events.

Westby (1984) has identified three patterns of difficulties in structuring oral narratives for children with language-learning disabilities. These patterns are:

1. **Inefficient processing**—Children with inefficient processing may be able to produce a narrative with appropriate macrostructure. However, these students may exhibit delayed

Narrative Toolbox

Table 4	**Story Grammar Development**	
Grade Level	**Story Grammar Level**	**Description**
Preschool	Descriptive Sequence	Descriptions of characters, surroundings, and usual actions of characters. No causal relationships or sequences of events are present. No clear story grammar elements are present.
Preschool	Action Sequence	Events in a chronological order with no causal relationships. Characters act independently of each other. No story grammar elements are present.
Preschool	Reactive Sequence	Contains causal relationships in that certain changes automatically cause other changes. There is no evidence of goal-directed behavior or planning behavior, but there is at least an initiating event and consequences. A setting and ending may also be introduced.
Early Elementary	Abbreviated Episode	Goal may be suggested or stated explicitly. The actions of the characters seem to be purposeful, but not as well thought out as in later stages. The story has an initiating event, an internal response, and a consequence. It may also have a statement of setting, a reaction to consequence, and an ending.
Early Elementary	Complete Episode	Relays an entire goal-oriented behavior. An initiating event, an internal response, attempt(s), and a consequence are required. The goals and intentions of the characters are apparent, and there is evidence of planning.
Late Elementary	Complex Episode	An elaboration of a complete episode with an additional partial or complete incident embedded in the episode. It could also contain multiple plans that are used to achieve a goal. Obstacles that hamper attainment of the goal are also shown.
Late Elementary	Multiple Episodes	Includes two or more episodes. The second episode follows the first one sequentially. All included episodes should be complete (by 10 years of age).
Late Elementary	Embedded Episodes	The most advanced use of story grammar. Includes at least two episodes whereby the first episode is interrupted by the second. After the second episode is concluded, the first episode continues.

Source: Glenn and Stein (1980)

responses, difficulty changing tasks, and slow retrieval of words. In addition, they may use vague vocabulary and frequently need repetitions and cues.

2. ***Inadequate organization***—These students may be characterized as possessing difficulties in planning a narrative. They may be able to answer questions appropriately about the characters' motivations and cause-effect relationships; however, their narratives are not organized in a logical, coherent manner. Narratives that lack organization may be only a sequence of statements; these stories lack a theme or plot and may include irrelevant details.

3. ***Insufficient schema knowledge***—Students with schema difficulties also have trouble with story planning. They may not be aware that the pictures in a book convey a story. They may describe each picture as a separate stimulus and misinterpret cause-effect and motivational relationships.

Students who demonstrate difficulty understanding and using narratives may also lack internal narrative skills, meaning those behaviors that help them monitor their own activities, express their feelings, empathize with others, and solve problems (Westby, 1991). Narrative deficits can have a profound effect on a student's ability to communicate, socialize, learn, and solve problems.

Developing Children's Narrative Skills

The development of oral narrative skills in early-elementary school helps children transition from oral language skills to written language skills (Westby, 1991). When narrative skills need to be specifically targeted to heighten students' understanding and use, the following four principles are important:

1. ***Exposure to well-formed literature and a literate style of language.*** Children who are exposed to well-formed narratives and literature become aware that these books and stories have a pattern. They recognize that there is a continuity to stories (i.e., the stories include a setting, a problem, a goal, and a series of events leading to a resolution of the problem or a conclusion). Unfortunately, many of the stories and books used in school, including basal readers, are not written to facilitate narrative development. "The majority of basal reading texts make minimal use of folk tales and well structured narratives" (Westby, 1984, p. 124).

2. ***Development of metanarrative awareness.*** Metanarrative awareness refers to the ability to talk about the structure and elements of a narrative and to manipulate this structure intentionally. Skilled communicators are aware of a listener's needs and will present, in a logical manner, a narrative that includes the setting and the events that occurred. The adept communicator may also be able to produce narratives with multiple character interactions and embedded episodes.

3. ***Use of scaffolding techniques by the educator to aid students in narrative construction.*** Through the use of scaffolding techniques, children can be taught strategies for developing and producing narratives. "Scaffolding is the use of leading questions that help the speaker organize his or her story" (Page and Stewart, 1985, p. 25). When exposed to scaffolding

strategies, a child learns narrative skills in contexts where a skilled language user provides the structure needed to complete the narrative. Verbal scaffolding can encourage a student to create a more complex story than he or she could create without help. By asking leading questions, the educator provides the scaffolding for the student to structure and sift through the linguistic context. Therefore, scaffolding questions should be slightly more advanced than the child's level of development (Applebee and Langer, 1983). Gradually, this framework can become internalized by the child, who is then able to generalize these skills without needing clarifying questions (i.e., scaffolds) from adults.

4. ***Use of graphic organizers to help students understand, structure, and remember narratives and specific story grammar elements.*** A graphic organizer is a mental or visual map that illustrates how information is arranged and organized. Such organizers allow students to see information as a set of relationships rather than as isolated facts. Through the repeated use of graphic organizers, students can learn to recognize these relationships without a visual representation. Organizers also help students simplify and make sense out of information contained in text. According to Flynn (1995), graphic organizers can help students:

   - Understand how information is connected

   - Understand and recall information

   - Organize observations, research, and opinions

   - Prepare written work and projects

   - Solve problems

   - Integrate thinking, reading, and writing processes

   - Apply higher level thinking skills to real-life situations

Assessing Narrative Skills

To determine if activities to enhance narrative development are needed, an assessment should be conducted. In such an evaluation, formal testing measures and informal procedures can be used. Two resources that include structured, more formal procedures for assessing a child's narrative skills are *Guide to Narrative Language: Procedures for Assessment* (Hughes et al., 1997) and *The Strong Narrative Assessment Procedure* (Strong, 1998). These resources give detailed information on how to collect, transcribe, and analyze narrative language samples.

Discussion related to conducting a thorough narrative assessment is beyond the scope of *Narrative Toolbox.* However, Appendix A provides a *Narrative Levels Analysis Form* that corresponds to the stages of narrative development described on pages 6–8. To complete Appendix A, check (✓) the student's mode of organization (e.g., heaps, sequences, complex stories) for each formulated task (i.e., original telling) and reformulated task (i.e., retelling) described. Include any other pertinent comments related to the student's performance.

Informal assessment measures are well suited for evaluating a student's level of narrative development (Westby, 1984). Informal procedures might include rubrics and rating scales.

Rubrics

A *rubric* is a coding system that includes a description of features against which to code a performance, behavior, or unit of language (Hughes et al., 1997). Rubrics provide a means for assigning qualitative values to various levels of student performance. With rubrics, students clearly understand what is expected of them because they are made aware of the layout of a rubric before it is used to judge their performance. Scores are earned and may translate into letter grades or point totals. Collecting rubrics throughout the school year is an excellent way to judge performance and document progress (or lack thereof). Rubrics serve not only as a scoring tool, but also as a means of illuminating areas in which further instruction may be necessary.

Appendix B includes two retelling rubrics for informally assessing children's narrative skills. *Retelling Rubric–1* can be used with younger elementary students or older students with limited narrative skills; *Retelling Rubric–2* can be used with older elementary students or those with more advanced narrative skills. These rubrics are designed along a story grammar framework. They include story grammar elements such as setting, first event, goal, plan, and outcome. Before introducing a story to use with a rubric, be sure the student is familiar with the rubric and the performance associated with each level. Also be certain to select a story that will present developmentally appropriate content, narrative structure, and story grammar elements. Read the story aloud and request the student to retell the story. Record the student's retelling so that it may be played back, if needed. Judge the student's performance using the selected rubric.

Two story creation rubrics are included in Appendix C. Creating an original story is a more challenging task than retelling a story since it requires the formulation of original thoughts as well as adherence to a story framework. *Story Creation Rubric–1* is intended for younger elementary students and older students with less-developed narrative skills. It includes some early-developing story grammar elements, such as setting (characters, time, and place) and solution. *Story Creation Rubric–2* is intended for older elementary students and those with more advanced narrative skills. This rubric includes all story grammar elements. When using a story creation rubric with a student, first be sure the student is familiar with the rubric and the performance associated with each level. Instruct the student to tell an original story in a format like one he or she might hear told from a book. Record the student's telling of the story so that it may be played back, if needed. Judge the student's story based on the selected rubric.

Discuss the scoring with individual students and other significant adults as appropriate. Keep completed rubrics in a student's file or portfolio for future reference. Re-administer a rubric whenever present level of performance information is needed.

Rating Scales

Rating scales, another way to informally measure a child's narrative skills, are qualitative guidelines that are often translated to numeric values. By completing a rating scale during an initial evaluation, re-administration of the scale at a later date can chart an individual student's development over time. Appendix D: *Story Rating Scale* is appropriate for use with students of any age.

Using *Narrative Toolbox*
Presenting the Lessons

Part 2 of this resource (beginning on page 21) includes an abundance of activities designed to help students understand and use critical story grammar elements and narrative skills. The lessons are divided into the following subsections: Introduction to Story Grammar Elements, Story Setting, Story Problem, Story Solution, Solving the Story Puzzle, and Written Narratives.

The activities in *Narrative Toolbox* are arranged as lessons in a recommended order of presentation. Due to the structured and sequential nature of narratives, students should be familiar with one story grammar element before the next in line is presented. However, the lessons provided should be supplemented with other activities or with an activity or discussion that may arise from a lesson in order to give students additional needed practice.

Each lesson in *Narrative Toolbox* includes one or more stated objectives, procedures for preparing materials, sample dialogue for introducing the lesson to students, activity instructions, and closing thoughts. The "Finishing Thoughts" section of each lesson includes sample dialogue to prompt a follow-up activity. These activities direct students to demonstrate or think about the newly learned concept in another situation or setting, which promotes generalization of skills. All lessons include reproducible materials, which are located immediately following the procedural information. It is best to read through a complete lesson before meeting with students so that the materials can be prepared and the recommended dialogue can be tailored to meet specific students' needs.

To help students develop heightened narrative skills, story grammar elements can be highlighted and practiced individually. This approach moves students from simple tasks to more challenging ones. In order to break a narrative into its specific story grammar elements, a task may become temporarily removed from a complete, true narrative. When this happens, students can better understand, question, and develop the particular story grammar element. This then adds to the students' conceptual framework for the comprehension and production of narratives. In *Narrative Toolbox,* the story grammar elements are isolated and practiced in the following order: setting (character, place, time), first event, response, goal, plan, attempt, outcome, and ending to correspond with the order they are typically found in a fictional story.

During some activities in *Narrative Toolbox,* students create and tell original stories. In other activities, students retell descriptions or stories modeled by the educator. When working with more than one student at a time, decide whether to use the same descriptions or stories with each student. Students can benefit from hearing one another's retellings and then attending to your feedback related to a retelling.

The activities included in *Narrative Toolbox* were designed based on the four principles described on pages 13–14: well-formed literature and a literate style of language, metanarrative awareness, scaffolding techniques, and graphic organizers. The application of these principles can be found in a variety of ways throughout the activities. The following restates each of these four principles and explains how each is infused into the *Narrative Toolbox* lessons.

1. ***Exposure to well-formed literature and a literate style of language.*** Throughout *Narrative Toolbox,* well-formed children's literature and a literate style of language are used to expose students to specific story grammar elements. These stories include those based on familiar trade books as well as original stories created for this resource. A list of recommended children's literature to use when helping students develop narrative skills is provided in Appendix E. Using trade books from students' general education curriculum and classroom is particularly advantageous. During the required activities, the books should be read aloud by the educator or students should listen to them on tape so that the emphasis of the activity is on narrative skill building rather than on reading. Shorter stories are recommended so that an activity can be completed in a single session. Stories should be able to be read in 10 minutes or less to allow for the remainder of the session to focus on the narrative development activity. Keep in mind that some story grammar elements are not clearly stated, but need to be inferred from the information in a story. Help students make these inferences when needed.

   Before reading a story with students, discuss the title and illustrations. Appendix F includes a list of helpful strategies to consider when reading stories aloud to students. Duplicate and enlarge this page and keep it posted in a location for easy reference when reading to students. Also before reading a story, establish a purpose for the task by talking to students about the information they can acquire from the story. While reading a story, stop occasionally to summarize what has happened and to predict what will happen next. Focus students' attention on new vocabulary, key events, and colorful phrases. Finally, after reading a story, reflect on the story's events and characters. Discuss any lessons learned or changes in the characters. Link the story and discussion to other children's books or classroom topics.

2. ***Development of metanarrative awareness.*** Metanarrative awareness is increased by talking with students about the structure and story grammar elements of a story. Sample dialogue is provided in all lessons to help students think and talk about narratives and story grammar elements. Modify the provided dialogue as needed. Allow the dialogue to turn into insightful discussions related to the targeted concept. Ask open-ended questions to stimulate discussion.

Narrative Toolbox

3. ***Use of scaffolding techniques by the educator to aid students in narrative construction.*** Scaffolding is provided by the educator to aid students in attaining higher level narrative skills. Appendix G presents scaffolding questions that can be used to help further students' narrative development. Notice that the questions are grouped to indicate which questions to use based on a student's present level of performance. After determining the level at which a student is producing narratives consistently, ask scaffolding questions from the appropriate group. For example, if a student is producing narratives that can be characterized as heaps, scaffolding questions such as "Who are the main characters in the story?" and "What happens in the story?" can be asked to help the student develop characters and create a central theme. As students become more adept at completing activities and telling stories, the use of scaffolding should be faded.

4. ***Use of graphic organizers to help students understand, structure, and remember narratives and specific story grammar elements.*** Graphic organizers are infused throughout the *Narrative Toolbox* lessons. The graphic organizers help students visualize, arrange, remember, and use the new concepts they are learning. The intended use of each visual tool is explained in the corresponding activity procedures. One graphic organizer that is used frequently is a story map, which is a visual depiction of a story. A story map illustrates the overall structure of the story and the inclusion of all the story grammar elements. Story maps have a variety of uses. They can be used to summarize a story after it is read, to plan a story prior to writing or telling it, and to retell a story. As students use story maps, they acquire a means for the interpretation of future stories. When students have a mental story map, they are prepared to arrange and categorize information from future stories or books they encounter. Figure 1 shows one version of a story map that is used throughout *Narrative Toolbox*. Two versions of a story map are located in Appendix H. Experiment with both maps to determine which one is more helpful to your students.

Figure 1 Story Map

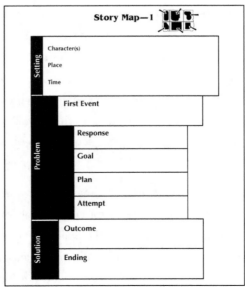

Transitioning to Written Narratives

In young children, oral language development leads to written language development. Later, oral language development slows and written language development comes to the forefront. The activities in *Narrative Toolbox* focus primarily on the development of oral narrative skills since students struggling with narrative development can benefit greatly from working at this level first. Even so, many writing opportunities are provided throughout the resource. When students need to focus more intently on written narrative skills, make the necessary adaptations to desired lessons. In addition, the last section of Part 2 includes activities that are specifically designed to target the development of written narrative skills.

Monitoring Progress

As students become more skilled at understanding and using narratives, it is important to monitor their development so that progress can be substantiated and future objectives can be identified. Student progress can be captured using several informal techniques, such as those that follow:

1. ***Have students self-report on their use of new skills in other situations.*** Remind students of the activity that was prompted by the previous lesson's "Finishing Thoughts" section, and have them discuss what they did. Having students self-report can be an insightful way to monitor their use of skills.

2. ***Re-administer one or more rubrics or a rating scale with a student.*** Having a student retell or tell a story, and then judging his or her performance using a rubric or rating scale provided in Appendices B, C, and D, is an excellent way to judge a child's skill development. Also, this method allows for a student's performance to be compared to how he or she performed on an earlier date.

3. ***Solicit input from other significant adults in a student's life.*** Using the *Feedback Form* in Appendix I, parents, teachers, and other adults can be asked to report on a student's understanding and use of specific concepts. Solicit feedback using this form whenever needed.

Rely on a combination of strategies for monitoring student progress. Keep in mind that the information collected should help document development and make decisions for future targets.

Final Thoughts

Enjoy the wealth of activities provided in *Narrative Toolbox*. This resource will become an irreplaceable tool as you help students construct story grammar knowledge and build narratives.

Lessons
Part 2

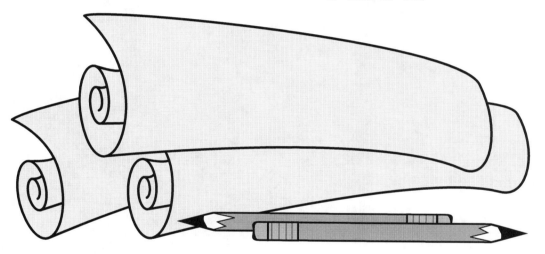

Introduction to Story Grammar Elements

Story Grammar Octopus 25
Story Train 30

Story Grammar Octopus

Objective

- Learn the labels for the following eight story grammar elements: *setting, first event, response, goal, plan, attempt, outcome,* and *ending*

Preparing Materials

1. Duplicate *Story Grammar Octopus* (page 28), one per student.

2. Duplicate *Story Grammar Octopus Tentacles* (page 29), one per student. Following along the lines, cut the pieces apart. (Have students do the cutting if appropriate.)

Preparing Students

Today let's think about some of the things we know that are made up of parts. For example, think about a bicycle. Let's tell some of the parts of a bicycle.

[Provide time for students to volunteer the names of various bicycle parts.]

As we can see, a bicycle is made up of many important parts. If any of these parts are missing, the bicycle would not work right. It might tip over, it might not move, or it might fall apart.

[If needed, discuss another item and its parts to further illustrate this concept.]

Another item that is made up of parts is a story. We will be learning about eight different parts that are needed to make a story. When all eight of these parts are included in a story, the story can be more interesting and easier to understand.

Activity Instructions

[Distribute one *Story Grammar Octopus* and one set of tentacles to each student. Have glue available.]

Each of you has a copy of an octopus. How many tentacles does the octopus have?

[Prompt a student to respond.]

Great! An octopus has eight tentacles. This is called a Story Grammar Octopus. Story grammar means the parts that make up a story. Do you remember I said that we would be talking about eight parts that make up a story? These parts are called story grammar elements. Each tentacle of the octopus will go along with a story grammar element. To help you start to learn these different story parts, I will read a description of each story grammar element out loud. While I am reading about each story grammar element, locate the part I am describing and set it into place on the octopus. When we have heard about each part, we will glue the pieces into place. Listen carefully to each description.

1. *The* setting *introduces, or begins, the story. It tells us three things: who the characters are in the story, where the story takes place, and when the story happens.* [Students should locate and place the Setting piece.]

2. *The* first event *is something that happens that begins the story. Everything that follows in the story is usually related to this first event.* [Students should locate and place the First event piece.]

3. *The* response *tells us how the first event changes the character. The response is usually how the character thinks or feels after the first event.* [Students should locate and place the Response piece.]

4. *The* goal *is what the character wants to happen. Sometimes the goal is easy to figure out. Sometimes the goal has to be figured out based on the character's actions in the story.* [Students should locate and place the Goal piece.]

5. *The* plan *is how the character tries to reach the goal. The plan might be very easy to identify, or we may need to figure out the plan from the events of the story.* [Students should locate and place the Plan piece.]

6. *The* attempt *is the character's actions to complete the plan. This is how the character tries to reach the goal.* [Students should locate and place the Attempt piece.]

7. *The* outcome *tells us if the attempt to complete the plan worked. The outcome is usually related to the first event that started the story.* [Students should locate and place the Outcome piece.]

8. *The* ending *tells us what happened last in the story.* [Students should locate and place the Ending piece.]

Now you should have all eight story grammar elements in place and your Story Grammar Octopus should be complete.

[Provide time for students to glue their pieces in place.]

When a story has all eight parts, we can call it a complete story. We will learn more about each of these eight story grammar elements using many different activities. We will practice by listening to stories, telling stories, and writing stories.

Finishing Thoughts

Take your Story Grammar Octopus *home and name the eight story parts to a friend or family member. While you read and listen to stories in your classroom and at home, think about all eight of these story grammar elements. Picture the* Story Grammar Octopus *in your mind, and try to find all eight parts in the story as you go along.*

Story Grammar Octopus

Name: _____ Date: _____

1. Listen to the description of each story grammar element.

2. Put each story grammar element into place on the octopus.

3. After all eight story grammar elements have been described, glue all the tentacles on the octopus.

Story Grammar Octopus Tentacles

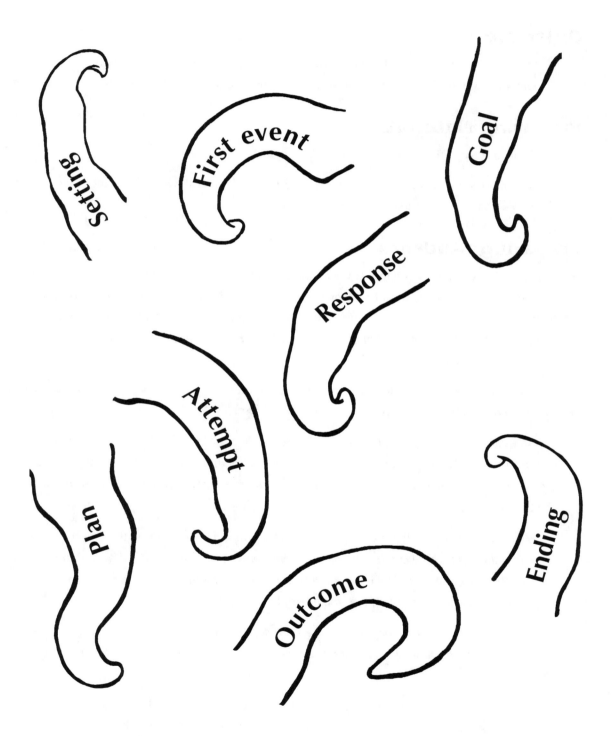

Story Train

Objective

- Group the story components (*character, place, time, first event, response, goal, plan, attempt, outcome,* and *ending*) into the following categories: Setting, Problem, Solution

Preparing Materials

1. Duplicate *Story Train* (page 32), one per student.

2. Duplicate *Story Train Pieces* (page 33), one per student. Following along the lines, cut the pieces apart. (Have students do the cutting if appropriate.)

Preparing Students

Using the Story Grammar Octopus, *we learned about the eight story grammar elements that can be found in a complete story. Many stories can be divided into three main sections: the Setting, the Problem, and the Solution. The Setting can go along with the beginning of the story, the Problem can be thought of as the middle of the story, and the Solution happens at the end of the story.*

[To illustrate these concepts, write the words *setting, problem,* and *solution,* paired with the words *beginning, middle,* and *end,* where everyone can see them.]

We can think of a story like a train. The Setting is usually described in the beginning of the story and can be thought of as the engine. The Setting tells us three story grammar elements: the characters, *or who is in the story; the* place, *or location, of the story; and the* time *of the story.*

The Problem comes about during the middle of the story, so it can be thought of as the boxcar of the train. There can be one or many problems in a story, just like there can be one or many boxcars in a train. The Problem tells us five story grammar elements: the first event, *the* response, *the* goal, *the* plan, *and the* attempt.

The Solution to a story happens at the end, so it is like the caboose of the train. The Solution tells us the last two story grammar elements: the outcome *and the* ending *of the story.*

[Sketch an outline of a train with three cars—engine, boxcar, caboose—where everyone can see it, and fill in the associated story grammar elements on each train car to further illustrate this concept, if needed. You may wish to erase the outline before beginning the next activity.]

Activity Instructions

[Distribute one *Story Train* and one set of train pieces to each student. Have glue available.]

Now that you're starting to understand the story grammar elements and the three different sections of a complete story, we'll practice grouping the story parts. Each of you has a blank Story Train *and some small paper train pieces that contain the story parts. You'll notice the parts include 7 story grammar elements and* character, place, *and* time. *That's because those three make up the Setting. Remember, the engine is like the Setting of the story, the boxcar is like the Problem in the story, and the caboose is like the Solution in the story. Listen to the following instructions to complete your* Story Train.

1. *Locate the* Character, Place, *and* Time *strips, and set them in the engine of the train. These parts make up the Setting of the story and usually come at the beginning, just like the engine comes at the beginning of the train.*

2. *Find the* First event, Response, Goal, Plan, *and* Attempt *strips, and set them in the boxcar of the train in that order.* [Repeat the order as necessary.] *These story grammar elements happen as the Problem in the story appears. This happens after the Setting, just like the boxcar comes after the engine in a train.*

3. *Set the* Outcome *and* Ending *strips into place in the caboose of the train. These two story grammar elements happen last as a result of the Problem being solved, so this section of the story can be thought of as the Solution. Since these story grammar elements come last, they are like the caboose of a train.*

[Provide time for students to glue their pieces into place.]

Finishing Thoughts

Today we learned that a story can have three main sections and that these sections are like the parts of a train. The Setting is like the train engine and includes the character, place, *and* time. *The Problem is like the boxcar of a train and includes the* first event, response, goal, plan, *and* attempt. *The Solution includes the* outcome *and* ending *of the story, so it is like the caboose of a train. Take your* Story Train *home and explain the different sections and parts to a friend or family member. Think about the three main sections of a story as you listen to or read a story.*

Story Train

Name: _____ Date: _____

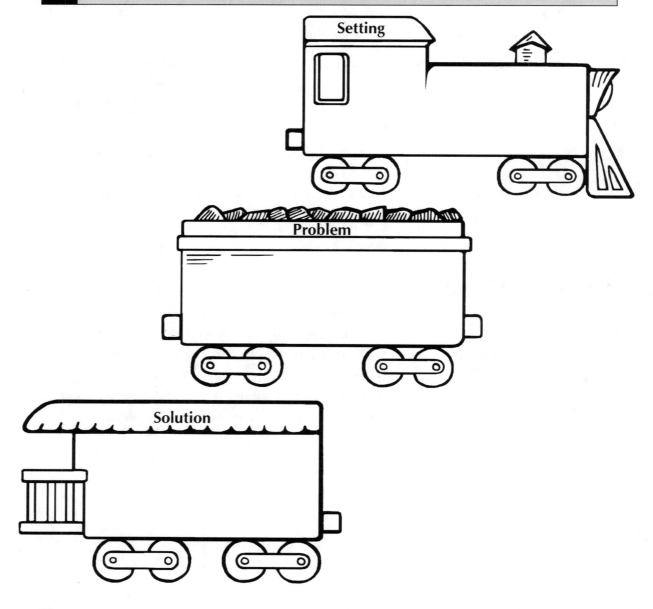

Story Train Pieces

Character	Place
Time	First event
Response	Goal
Plan	Attempt
Outcome	Ending

Story Setting

Character

Character Descriptions...37

Character Changes..42

Character Comparison 46

Additional Character Activities...49

Place

Place Comparison...50

Creating a Mood..53

Setting the Stage..59

Additional Place Activities 62

Time

Time Machines...63

Time Chance..67

Additional Time Activities..70

Character Descriptions

Objective

- Produce at least five relevant descriptive statements during a retelling of a character description

Preparing Materials

1. Duplicate *Story Scene—Jungle* and *Story Scene—Bedroom* from Appendix J (pages 193–194). Color the two scenes and mount them on poster board. If desired, laminate the colored pictures for durability. The scenes for this activity should be appropriate for most students; if not, draw or locate alternate scenes.

2. Locate a Tarzan-like figurine for the jungle scene and a boy figurine for the bedroom scene. Use figurines found at discount stores or garage sales, or use those provided in kids' meals from fast-food restaurants. If the precise figurine cannot be located, direct children to use their imaginations to pretend that a substitute figurine is a particular character. If scenes other than the jungle and the bedroom are being used, locate appropriate figurines.

3. Duplicate *Retelling Form—Jungle Scene* and *Retelling Form—Bedroom Scene* (pages 39–40), one per student. (Depending on time and interest, you may wish to have students use only one form.) Complete the Name and Date portions of the forms before meeting with students. If scenes other than those provided are being used, use *Retelling Form—Blank* (page 41) to create a customized form.

Preparing Students

Look at these colorful scenes. Can anyone tell me the place you see in each scene?

[Provide time for students to volunteer the names of the scenes.]

Right, one is a jungle and one is a bedroom. I have one character that belongs in each scene. Character *might be a new word for you. Who can guess what the word* character *means?*

[Provide time for students to volunteer ideas.]

A character is a person or an animal that has a part in a story. For the jungle scene, the character I have is Tarzan. For the bedroom scene, I have a little boy character. We will call him Martin. Today I am going to tell you a short story about each character. In a complete story, it is important that each character is described. This helps people understand and enjoy the story. You will get a chance to tell about these characters today.

Activity Instructions

There are many different things you can say about a character. For example, you can tell about how characters look, what they enjoy doing, how old they are, and what their families are like. Think about all the kinds of things you know about the characters in some of your favorite stories or shows. You know these things because the story tells them to you or because of what the characters do during the story.

[Take time to talk about the things students know about some of their favorite story characters.]

Listen closely as I tell about Tarzan in the jungle.

[While using the Tarzan figurine, read the short character description provided in the shaded box on *Retelling Form—Jungle Scene.*]

Now listen closely as I tell about Martin in his bedroom.

[While using the boy figurine, read the short character description provided in the shaded box on *Retelling Form—Bedroom Scene.*]

[Following each character description, direct a student to conduct the task in a similar way. Using the student's *Retelling Form*s, transcribe the student's descriptions and indicate the number of sentences in the blank provided. (Audiotape the student's description and transcribe it at a later time, if desired.) Provide each student with at least one turn to tell about a character following your description. Review completed forms with students, and save them in student files or portfolios.]

Finishing Thoughts

Today we learned what a character in a story is and how important it is to make sure you explain about a character when you're telling a story. This makes a story more interesting, and it makes it easier to understand what happens in a story. The next time you listen to a story, pick your favorite character and think about everything the story tells you about that character. Remember, your favorite character might be an animal instead of a person!

Retelling Form—Jungle Scene

Name: _____   Date: _____

> Tarzan lives in the jungle. He lives with a gorilla family. Tarzan swings on vines in the trees. Tarzan walks like a gorilla. Once, when a tiger attacked the gorillas, Tarzan killed the tiger. Tarzan is very brave and strong. He likes to eat bananas and drink coconut milk.

Student's Character Description:

_____

_____

_____

_____

_____

_____

_____

Number of Sentences: _____

Retelling Form—Bedroom Scene

Name: _____   Date: _____

> Martin was very excited. He was finally going to have a bedroom all to himself. Martin's older brother, Diego, was going away to college, so Martin would not have to share a bedroom with Diego anymore. Martin loves baseball, dinosaurs, and music, so he decided to hang his baseball posters on the wall, set his dinosaur books on the dresser, and play his music without his headphones on.

Student's Character Description:

_____

_____

_____

_____

_____

_____

_____

Number of Sentences: _____

Retelling Form—Blank

Name: _____   Date: _____

Original Character Description: _____

_____

_____

_____

_____

_____

Student's Character Description:

_____

_____

_____

_____

_____

_____

_____

Number of Sentences: _____

Character Changes

Objective

- Identify whether a character is a flat character (i.e., he or she does not change during the course of a story) or a round character (i.e., he or she changes during the course of a story) and if round, identify the factors that caused the character to change

Preparing Materials

1. Locate two children's books to read aloud to students. One book should have a character that does not change during the story, and the other book should contain a character that changes during the story. Recommended flat character stories include:

   The Mitten: A Ukranian Folk Tale (1989)   *Who Is the Beast?* (1994)
   by Jan Brett   by Keith Baker
   New York: Putnam   New York: Voyager

   Recommended round character stories include:

   Big Bad Bruce (1982)   *The Rainbow Fish* (1996)
   by Bill Peet   by Marcus Pfister
   Boston: Houghton Mifflin   New York: North-South Books

2. Duplicate *Flat Character Form* (page 44) and *Round Character Form* (page 45), one per student.

Preparing Students

We are going to learn more about characters. Since characters are people or animals, we know that they can change as time goes by and as things happen to them. We are going to talk about characters that change during a story and characters that don't change during a story.

A flat character does not change during a story, just like the direction of your pencil would not change if you were drawing a flat line.

[Demonstrate this drawing motion where everyone can see.]

No matter what happens, who the character meets, or where the character goes, the personality of the character stays the same. You know that a character is a flat character if the words you would use to describe the character at the beginning of the story are the same as the words you would use to describe that character at the end of the story.

A round character changes during a story, just like the direction of your pencil would change if you were drawing a round circle.

[Demonstrate this drawing motion where everyone can see.]

A round character may change because of the events in the story or because of another character. Sometimes characters face a challenging situation or problem and they end up learning a lesson. A round character can change in a positive way, like becoming kind to others, or in a negative way, like developing a bad habit. You know that a character is a round character if the words you would use to describe the character at the beginning of the story are different from the words you would use to describe the character at the end of the story.

Activity Instructions

To think and talk about flat and round characters, I will read you two different stories. In one story, there is a character that does not really change. In the other story, there is a character that does change. Listen to each story and think carefully about the main characters. See if you can tell whether these characters are changing during the story. Think about how you would describe each character at the beginning of the story, and then how you would describe each character at the end of the story. If your description does not change, that would mean the character is a flat character. If your description does change, that would mean the character is a round character. After each story, you will be asked to complete a description of two characters—a flat character and a round character.

[Read the two selected stories to students. Highlight various character elements as necessary. Distribute one *Flat Character Form*, one *Round Character Form*, and a pen or pencil to each student.]

Great listening! It was interesting to hear about two different types of characters in those stories. Your job is to decide which character was a flat character and which character was a round character. Use the page with the long line at the top to tell about a flat character. Use the page with the circle at the top to tell about a round character. Ask questions if you don't understand something on a page.

[Provide students with time to complete the *Flat Character Form* and *Round Character Form*. Provide assistance to students as needed. Consider completing one set of pages aloud, as a group, if students need assistance with reading or writing skills. Review the pages when students are finished.]

Finishing Thoughts

Take your character pages home and share them with a friend or family member. Teach that person the difference between a flat character and a round character. Think about a character in the next story you read or hear. Decide whether that character is a flat character or a round character.

Flat Character Form

Name: _____ Date: _____

At the beginning of the story, _____ was

(character's name)

_____

_____

_____.

(character description)

At the end of the story, _____ was

(character's name)

_____

_____

_____.

(character description)

_____ **DID NOT CHANGE** during

(Character's name)

the story, so he/she is a **FLAT** character.

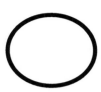

Round Character Form

Name: _____ Date: _____

Instructions

1. Listen to the story.

2. Choose a character that DOES CHANGE during the story.

3. Fill in the blanks with information about that ROUND character.

At the beginning of the story, _____ was
(character's name)

_____

_____

_____.
(character description)

At the end of the story, _____ was
(character's name)

_____

_____

_____.
(character description)

_____ **DID CHANGE** during the
(Character's name)

story, because _____

_____

_____

_____, so he/she is a **(ROUND)** character.
(reason for the change)

Character Comparison

Objective

- Compare themselves to a character in a story based on information that is stated or inferred

Preparing Materials

1. Locate an appropriate book to read aloud to students. Refer to the literature list in Appendix E (page 183) for recommended titles.

2. Duplicate *Character Comparison* (page 48), one per student.

Preparing Students

We have learned many things about the characters in stories. We know how important it can be to use clear character descriptions when we tell a story. It is also important to pay attention to the details we learn about characters when we listen to a story. We know that this information can help us understand a story. Sometimes you might hear or read a story and feel connected with a particular character. The character might be like you in some way; like he or she might be your age, or the character might be someone you think is really special. When you read or hear a story, you might try to compare the character to yourself. Compare means to tell how things are alike and how they are different. You might also try to compare two characters in the same story or compare two characters from two different stories. When we compare things and find their likenesses and differences, we can better understand them.

Activity Instructions

Today I will read a story. As you listen to the story, be sure to pay attention to what you learn about the characters. Think about whether one of the characters is like you in any way. Think about if one of the characters is someone you would choose as a friend. Pay attention to all the details that describe the characters and to all the action that happens to the characters.

[Read the story aloud to students. If students have more advanced reading skills, consider having students read stories on their own. After the story is read, distribute one copy of *Character Comparison* and a pen or pencil to each student.]

Look at this page. You will notice empty boxes and circles on the page. The first thing you need to do is choose a character from the story you just listened to. Write your name and the character's name in the top two boxes. Then tell all you can about how you and the character are alike. Write these ideas in the large rectangle. Next think of the ways you and the character are different from each other. Write those ideas in the circles on the page.

[Provide students with time to complete their pages. Review completed pages as a group.]

Finishing Thoughts

When you take your Character Comparison *page home, explain the information to a friend or family member. See how much information you can remember about the character in the story by explaining how this character is like you and different from you. Next time you read or listen to a story, think about how a character in the story is the same as or different from you.*

Character Comparison

Name: _____ Date: _____

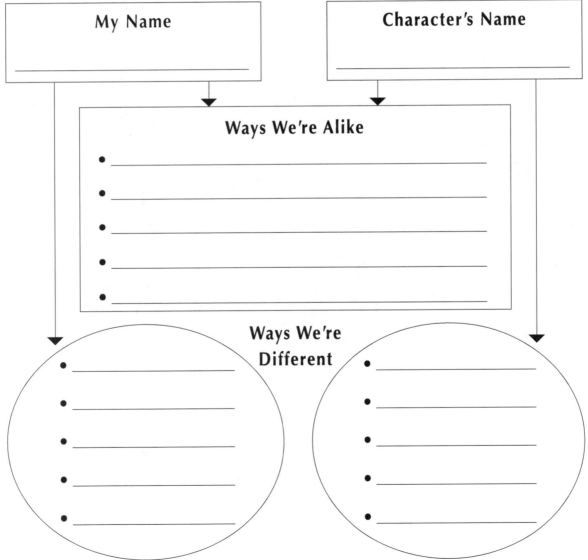

My Name	Character's Name
_____	_____

Ways We're Alike

- _____
- _____
- _____
- _____
- _____

Ways We're Different

- _____
- _____
- _____
- _____
- _____

- _____
- _____
- _____
- _____
- _____

Additional Character Activities

Educator Note

Some students may need additional practice in understanding and using the *character* component of the Setting category. Assigning one of the following activities may be helpful. For the most effective use of these activities, use trade books from students' general education curricula, or books students are reading for leisure.

Activities

1. Describe or draw the most important character in the story. Tell why you consider this character to be the most important.

2. Write a character's name and then think of an attribute or action that starts with each letter of his or her name that also describes the character. For example, in the book *Charlotte's Web,* the words **W**ishful, **I**nterested, **L**oving, **B**ashful, **U**seful, and **R**enowned could be used to describe the character Wilbur the pig.

3. Describe or draw your favorite character in the story. Tell why this character is your favorite.

4. Describe or draw your least favorite character in the story. Tell why this character is your least favorite.

5. Tell about something a character did that you agreed with or disagreed with. If you disagree with what the character did, explain what you would have done in the same situation.

6. Talk about a feeling that a character had that you have also felt. Explain what might have made the character feel this way; then explain what made you feel the same way.

7. Attempt to guess why a character acted in a certain way. Describe the situation that happened.

8. Tell if there was a character in the story that you felt sorry for. Explain what made you feel sad for the character. What do you wish would have happened instead?

9. Tell about a character in the story that reminds you of a character you know from another story, TV show, or movie. What makes these characters similar? Are they different in any ways? If so, how?

10. Tell about a character in the story that reminds you of someone you know. What makes these people similar? Are they different in any ways? If so, how?

11. Does the author come right out and tell you about the character's thoughts and feelings? Or do you have to guess what a character thinks and feels based on his or her actions?

12. Create a paper doll of a character from the story. Design an outfit that the paper doll character could wear. Use the paper doll as a bookmark.

Place Comparison

Objective

- Compare the location in which a story takes place with the place in which they live

Preparing Materials

1. Locate an appropriate book to read aloud to students. Refer to the literature list in Appendix E (page 183) for recommended titles.

2. Duplicate *Place Comparison* (page 52), one per student.

Preparing Students

We know that the word place *means the location of something. So, the place of a story means the location of where it happens, such as the planet, the country, the state, the city, the neighborhood, the building, or the room where the story takes place. Think about where one of your favorite stories takes place.*

[Provide students with time to share the locations of their favorite stories.]

How do you know it takes place in that location? Is it because the story tells you the place or because the pictures show you the place or do you know by clues that are in the story?

[Provide time for students to respond.]

We can understand the place of the story through many different clues that might be in the story. The author's description of the weather, the people, and the surroundings can help us decide where a story takes place. The pictures can also help us understand the place. Both the character information and place information are part of the Setting and usually come at the beginning of the story, even though they can change as the story goes along. The place information helps us start to understand the story. Remember, the place can change and there can be one, two, or many places in a single story. Think about all the places you might go in a single day. The story of your day might take place in many different locations. When a story changes place, it can sometimes be difficult to understand or explain these changes. It's important to practice identifying and talking about the different places in a story.

Activity Instructions

I am going to read a story. As you listen to the story, be sure to pay attention to what you learn about the location of the story. Think about whether the place stays the same during the whole story or if the place changes. Think about how the place or places in the story are alike and different from the places you visit in your life.

[Read the story aloud to students. If students have more advanced reading skills, consider having students read stories on their own. After the story is read, distribute one copy of *Place Comparison* and a pen or pencil to each student.]

Look at this page. You will notice empty boxes and circles on the page. The first thing you need to do is choose a place from the story you just heard. Write the name of a place in your life and the name of a place from the story in the designated boxes. Then tell all you can about how these two places are alike. Write these ideas in the large rectangle. Next think of the ways these places are different from each other. Write those ideas in the circles on the page.

[Provide students with time to complete their pages. Review completed pages as a group.]

Finishing Thoughts

When you take your Place Comparison *page home, explain the information to a friend or family member. See how much information you can remember about the place in the story by explaining how it is alike and different from a place in your life. Next time you read or listen to a story, think about how a place in the story is alike or different from a place you know well. Next time you tell a story, remember to think and tell about the places the characters go.*

Place Comparison

Name: _____   Date: _____

1. Listen to the story.
2. Choose a place from the story.
3. Fill in the blanks with information comparing a place you know well to a place you selected from the story.

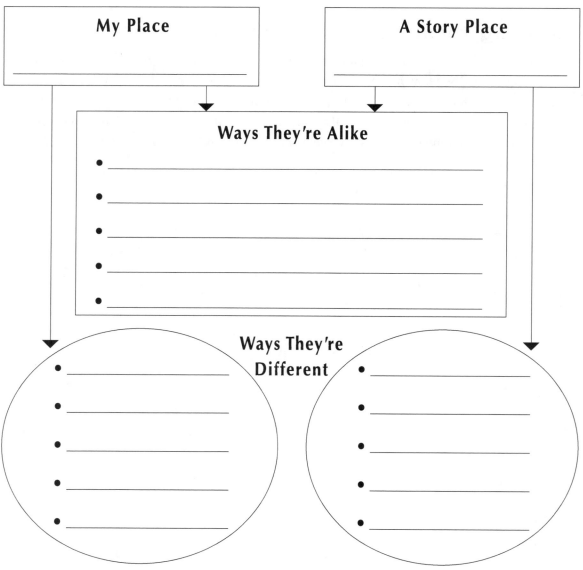

My Place	A Story Place
_____	_____

Ways They're Alike

*   _____
*   _____
*   _____
*   _____
*   _____

Ways They're Different

*   _____
*   _____
*   _____
*   _____
*   _____

*   _____
*   _____
*   _____
*   _____
*   _____

Creating a Mood

Objective

- Identify the mood of a situation based on the place where it occurs

Preparing Materials

1. Duplicate *Place Cards* and *Mood Cards* (pages 55–58).

2. Cut the cards apart and set the stack of Place cards and the stack of Mood cards in the center of a playing surface.

Preparing Students

The author of a story can use words and descriptions to create the mood of the story. The mood is the feeling you get when you hear or read the story. For example, a mystery story may take place in a dark, haunted, empty mansion. As the characters roam through the house, you might be able to feel the mood of suspense and mystery.

If you heard that a story took place in a crowded school gym during the most important basketball game of the year, what kind of mood might you feel?

[Provide time for students to respond and to discuss the mood of the hypothetical story.]

What about if a story took place in a hospital as two ambulances full of injured people arrived at the emergency room? What kind of mood might that create?

[Provide time for students to respond and to discuss the mood of the hypothetical story.]

The mood is an important part of a story that is often expressed through the place of a story. Being able to understand the mood is just one great reason to pay attention to the clues that show the location in which a story takes place.

Activity Instructions

We are going to play a card game to help us recognize story places and the moods the places might express. You will notice two stacks of cards in front of us. One stack of cards includes descriptions of story locations. Those are the same as the place story grammar element. The other stack of cards describes different moods. We will try to match one Mood card to each Place card. Sometimes there might be a Mood card that could go with more than one Place Card or a Place card that could go with more than one Mood card. That's okay. Let's see how many matches we can make.

Narrative Toolbox

[One at a time, turn over a *Place Card,* have students read it aloud, and lay it faceup next to the previous card. Once all the *Place Cards* have been turned over, continue to sort through the *Mood Cards* with students, helping them identify matches. As alternates for playing this game, consider shuffling all the cards together and using them in a traditional game of Go Fish or Memory.]

Finishing Thoughts

Pay attention to the mood that is felt in all the different places you visit each day. Whenever you're in a place that has a certain mood, tell a friend or family member about the mood you feel. Explain why the particular place has a certain mood. The next time you hear or read a story, think about the place and the mood you feel. Remember that both the mood and the place in the story might change as the story goes along. The next time you tell a story, try to create a certain mood by the description you give of the places in the story.

Place Cards

In a dark, howling cave	**At an important basketball game**
Stranded on a cold mountaintop	**In your house during a thunderstorm**
Outside in a snowstorm	**At your desk taking a difficult test**
At your birthday party	**At the theater watching a funny movie**

Place Cards

At the supper table with your family	**At the animal shelter choosing a new puppy**
On the beach lying in the warm sand	**At the library reading a book**
In line waiting to get a flu shot	**At the zoo on a summer day**
In a fancy restaurant with your family	**At the store waiting in a long line just to buy a pack of gum**

Mood Cards

fearful	**excited**
lonely	**worried**
panicked	**stressful**
joyful	**silly**

Mood Cards

loving	confused
relaxed	quiet
nervous	busy
proud	bothered

Setting the Stage

Objective

- Identify and describe the *place* component of the setting story grammar element of a story

Preparing Materials

1. Locate several children's books, one to read aloud to students. (NOTE: Choose books that focus a fair amount of attention on the *place* story grammar element.) Refer to the literature list in Appendix E (page 183) for recommended titles.

2. Duplicate *Setting the Stage* (page 61), one per student.

Preparing Students

We know that the setting of a story describes the characters and the place. A story may take place in one location or in many different locations. The description of the place sets the backdrop for the events in a story, just as the items on a stage set the backdrop for a play. Think of a play you have seen. What sorts of items were on the stage that helped you understand where the play or the scene was taking place?

[Provide time for students to respond.]

So, we know that the items on a stage can help us understand the location of a play, just like the words an author uses can help us understand where a story takes place. Many authors describe the location so well that you can form a picture of the place in your mind. Let's look through some of these books to see if we can find the words that describe the place of the story.

[Look through several books with students, identifying place descriptions.]

Remember, a story's place can change as the story goes along, so you might find that an author is describing different places at various times during the story. That means that we need to listen for place descriptions throughout the whole story.

Activity Instructions

[Distribute one copy of *Setting the Stage* and a pen or pencil to each student.]

I will read a story out loud, and I want you to listen to the author's words that tell us about a place where the story happens. Pretend the story is going to be performed as a play on a stage, like the stage you see on the paper in front of you. As you listen to the story, think about a place that is being described. Pay special attention if the story changes place as it goes along. More than one place might be described in the story. After I read the story one time, think of a place that was described in the story.

[Read the selected story aloud to students. Read through any place clues slowly, pausing for students to have time to process the information.]

Now I will read the story a second time while you draw the scenery that shows one of the places from the story. Listen for words or phrases in the story that give you clues about a place in the story. When you have finished drawing a place, write the clues on the lines provided below the stage.

[Read the story a second time while students complete their *Setting the Stage* pages. Take time to discuss the story's place(s) and the clues that describe the place(s).]

Finishing Thoughts

Please take your Setting the Stage *pages home to share with a friend or family member. The scene you drew and the clues you listed will help you describe the* place *story grammar element to a person who has not heard the story. Maybe this will also help you tell the entire story to this person. Remember to listen for place clues whenever you hear or read a story. These clues can help you understand a story. Also remember to use place clues whenever you tell a story. Then the person listening to you will enjoy your story even more!*

Setting the Stage

Name: _____ Date: _____

1. Listen to the story.
2. Choose a place that is described in the story.
3. Draw a picture on the stage that shows the place you selected.
4. Fill in the Place Clues at the bottom of the page with words or ideas from the story that helped you draw your picture.

Place Clues

1. _____

2. _____

3. _____

Additional Place Activities

Educator Note

Some students may need additional practice in understanding and using the *place* component of the Setting category. Assigning one of the following activities may be helpful. For the most effective use of these activities, use trade books from students' general education curricula, or books students are reading for leisure.

Activities

1. Tell a story of your typical school day. List all the places you go. Check your list so that you remember to give clear place descriptions.

2. Pretend one of your favorite stories was changed to take place in your own neighborhood. Describe how the events of the story might happen differently because of this change of place.

3. On a large sheet of paper, draw all the different places that are described within a single story. Draw the places in the order in which they appear in the story.

4. Choose one of your favorite places to visit. Draw a picture of that place, showing all the detail you can think of. Next tell a story about that place. Look at your drawing while telling the story so that you remember to describe the place and all its details.

5. Describe how the characters in one of your favorite stories feels about the location of the story. Explain the character's emotions and why the place might make the character feel that way. Then describe your emotions about the different places you go during a typical day.

6. Look through a book you haven't read before (be sure the book has many pictures). Without reading the words, try to decide the places that are part of the story. Then read or listen to the story and see if your place guesses were right. Compare the words the author uses in the story to the pictures that appear. Do the pictures help you figure out the different places that are described?

Time Machines

Objective

- Identify when a story takes place

Preparing Materials

1. Duplicate *Time Machines* (page 66), one per student.

Preparing Students

The time of the story tells us when a story takes place. The author usually tells us the time of the story at the beginning. Together, character, place, *and* time *make up the Setting of the story.*

A story that occurs in the past could have happened yesterday, last week, last month, last year, or many years ago. Think of a story that takes place in the past.

[Provide time to talk about a story that takes place in the past.]

If a story is happening now, it is happening in the present. Let's think of a story that takes place in the present.

[Provide time to talk about a story that takes place in the present.]

A story that takes place tomorrow, next week, next year, or many years from now is set in the future. The future is a time that hasn't happened yet. Who can name a story that occurs in the future?

[Provide time to talk about a story that takes place in the future.]

Knowing when a story takes place helps us know more about the story. It might also give us a clue as to what the story will be about. For example, a story that takes place in the future might take place in space and have nonhuman creatures, and a story that takes place in the past might be about a famous event in history.

Let's practice thinking about the time *of a story. I am going to tell you the beginning of three different stories. Use the words* past, present, *or* future *to tell when each story might be taking place.*

- *The residents of the colony on Saturn anxiously awaited the arrival of the space shuttle.* [future]

- *On the grassy field, the knights in their battle armor nervously faced each other, clutching their jousts.* [past]

- *Tony decided to take his skateboard to the park on a sunny day.* [present]

Narrative Toolbox

What clues did you have about the time each story might be taking place? Since you only heard one sentence from each story, you were not told specifically when the story was taking place. You needed to guess from the clues. Sometimes we need to figure out the time of a story from clues, and sometimes the author will come right out and tell us the time of the story.

Activity Instructions

[Distribute one copy of *Time Machines* and a pen or pencil to each student.]

You will notice that you have three different time machines on your papers. The time machine on top goes to the past. The time machine in the middle is for the present. The time machine on the bottom of the page goes to the future. You will get to listen to three short stories. As you listen to each story, think about the time words and clues to decide whether the story is taking place in the past, present, or future. Then write the name of the story and at least one character from the story in the appropriate time machine. For example, if you decide that a story takes place in the past, write the name of the story and the name of at least one character from the story in the time machine that is on the top of the page. Listen carefully to each story. We'll talk about your answers after we do all three stories.

[Read the following three stories. As you begin to read each story, write its name where everyone can see it. Pause as needed for students to fill in their *Time Machines* pages.]

Story #1—The Computer Scare

As the computer warmed up, Cheng and Jack pulled another chair up to the computer. Cheng logged in and Jack opened his notebook. Their paper was due next hour, so they had to finish it right away. Mr. Rodriguez did not like late papers, especially not papers that had been assigned two weeks in advance. While Cheng put the floppy disk into the computer, Jack found the rough draft in his notebook. "Jack, where is our paper? I can't find it on the disk," Cheng said with a nervous voice. "It has to be on that disk. That's the one I used," Jack replied. "Jack, I have looked through the files one by one. It is not on this disk. Didn't you save it?" Cheng questioned. "No, I thought you saved it last time," Jack cried. At that moment, Mr. Rodriguez walked by and noticed the boys panicking. "Can I help you guys out?" he asked. "We can't find our paper on the disk. I guess we forgot to save it last time," Cheng said. "Fortunately, I know a little about computers, so I think I can help you," Mr. Rodriguez replied. In a short time, Mr. Rodriguez found a backup file and the boys were able to finish their paper on time. Both boys admitted that they could have avoided this panic if they had finished their paper sooner.

Story #2—Searching for Water

The inhabitants of Earth were worried. Years of widespread pollution had damaged the air, water, and other natural resources. Food and clean drinking water were very difficult to find. A group of space travelers were preparing to search other planets in the galaxy for food and water. A small dog named Stevie would be joining the expedition. Stevie would try any water the expedition found. If the water was safe for Stevie, then it would be brought back to Earth to be tested. The brave group explored throughout the galaxy. They found a hidden planet that looked remarkably like Earth. The planet had a large water supply and was lush with fruits and vegetables. The space travelers held their breath as Stevie lapped some water from a pond. Stevie quickly drank the water and seemed fine. The group cheered and collected as much water as they could for the return trip to Earth.

Story #3—A Ride in the Country

As her father held the reins, Betty carefully mounted her horse. Her mother ran out of the house with Betty's lunch pail and school books tied together with a belt. "Now, don't dawdle on your way to school," her mother reminded. "Yes, Mother, I'll be on time today," Betty promised. With her parents waving good-bye, Betty clicked to the horse and headed to town. Betty plodded along the country road, enjoying the sunshine and the warm breeze. A loud noise and the smell of smoke interrupted her thoughts. In the distance, Betty could make out something coming toward her on the road. Straining her eyes to see it, Betty laughed to herself in delight. It was a car. She had heard that her neighbors had bought a car. It was the only one in town. As the car went past her, Betty smiled and waved. "Someday," she thought, "maybe I will be able to ride to school in a car."

[Provide time for students to complete their *Time Machines* pages. Discuss their answers.]

Finishing Thoughts

Take your Time Machines *pages home and share them with a friend or family member. Try to use the information you wrote in each time machine to tell each short story you heard. The* time, place, *and* character *story clues can help you tell the stories. Next time you listen to, read, or tell a story, listen for time words and clues so that you can understand the story better or make your story clearer.*

Time Machines

Name: _____ Date: _____

Instructions	1. Listen to each story.
	2. Decide the time each story takes place.
	3. Fill in the blanks of each time machine with the name of the story that takes place in that time and at least one character from the story.

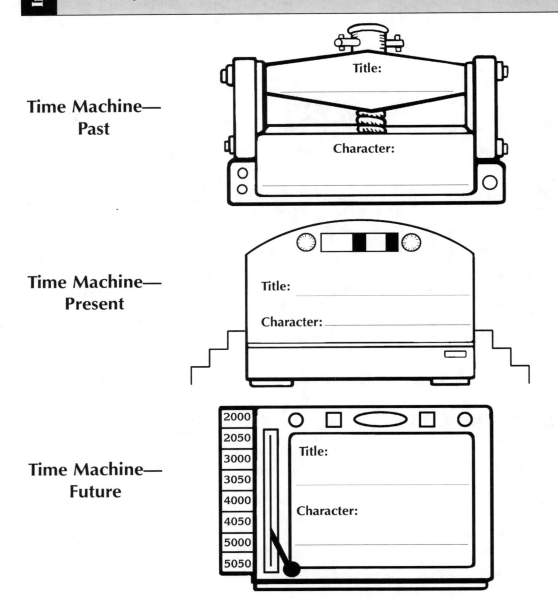

Time Machine— Past

Title:

Character:

Time Machine— Present

Title:

Character:

Time Machine— Future

Title:

Character:

Time Chance

Objective

- Produce the beginning of a narrative with reference to the time the story occurs

Preparing Materials

1. Duplicate *Time Chance Guide* (page 69), one per student. (Or enlarge and duplicate one copy for everyone to refer to while playing the game.)

2. Locate one standard die per student. (Or have the group share a die.)

Preparing Students

We know that the time in a story tells us when the events take place. The time in a story can be the time on a clock, such as 9:30, or it can be a certain day, month, season, or year. Here are a few examples of some different times that can be mentioned in a story:

[Write the following words where everyone can see them.]

- *Time on a clock (like noon, 3:30, or in 10 minutes)*
- *Days (like Saturday, yesterday, or my birthday)*
- *Months (like October, next month, or July)*
- *Seasons (like fall, winter, or spring)*
- *Years (like last year, two years ago, or 2010)*

The time may stay the same during a story, or a story may be spread across time. When you understand the time of a story, the story will be easier to understand and learn from. By talking about time when you tell a story, other people will be able to follow along easier.

Activity Instructions

[Distribute one *Time Chance Guide* and one die to each student.]

Today we are going to play a game called Time Chance to practice beginning a story and telling about the time of a story. We will take turns creating story starters by making up the first couple of lines of stories, being sure to tell when the story takes place. Since we've also learned that character and place ideas are also usually mentioned at the beginning of a story, your story starter might include these details too. For example, you might start a story by saying, "Yesterday, while he was walking past the school, Juan fell into the biggest hole that he had ever seen."

Narrative Toolbox

The character was Juan; the place was near the school; and the time was yesterday. Before you tell your story starter, you will need to shake your die. Then look at your Time Chance Guide to see what type of time you should include in your story starter. For example, if the die lands on 1, you need to give a story starter that includes a specific hour, such as "My dad arrived home from work at 6:00. He seemed more tired than usual." If the die lands on 2, you need to include a specific day in your story starter, such as "Last Thursday, our class heard a strange noise coming from the music room." We'll keep going until everyone has had at least a couple of turns to make up a story starter.

[Play Time Chance until each student has had at least three turns to create a story starter. Assist students by providing scaffolding cues as needed.]

Finishing Thoughts

Now you can take your Time Chance Guides home and play the game with a friend or family member. Be sure to explain the rules to all the players before you begin. Remember to listen for time clues whenever you read or listen to a story and to mention the time whenever you tell a story. Have fun playing Time Chance!

Time Chance Guide

If you roll a:

Create a story starter that talks about an HOUR.

Create a story starter that talks about a DAY.

Create a story starter that talks about a MONTH.

Create a story starter that talks about a SEASON.

Create a story starter that talks about a YEAR.

Create a story starter that talks about ANY TIME.

Additional Time Activities

Educator Note

Some students may need additional practice in understanding and using the *time* component of the Setting category. Assigning one of the following activities may be helpful. For the most effective use of these activities, use trade books from students' general education curricula, or books students are reading for leisure.

Activities

1. Describe how time progresses in a story. Do the events occur in the order in which they happened? Does the author jump between the past and the present? Does the author jump between the present and the future?

2. Tell how the author shows the passage of time. Are clues like descriptions and pictures used? Or does the author come right out and tell you when the story events are happening?

3. Change the time in one of your favorite stories to happen 50 years in the future or 200 years in the past. How might the story be different? Would the story be the same in any way? Draw a picture of a scene from the story as you think about the change in time.

4. As you are making up a new story, decide if the time of the story plays an important part. For example, does something need to get accomplished by a certain time? Does the time determine the types of characters and events that appear in the story? Or could your story be basically the same regardless of when it takes place?

5. Sketch out a story using a timeline. On several sheets of paper taped side by side, write or draw details from the story that show the story's progression. Make notes that show the time along the way.

6. Look through a storybook that has pictures. Without reading the words, try to determine the time the story takes place. Can you tell by the pictures if the time changes during the story? Talk about the different types of time that are easy to notice in pictures (like seasons) and the types of time that are difficult to tell from pictures (like day of the week).

Story Problem

Introduction to the Story Problem 73

First Event Categories 76

First Event Scripts 81

Response Card Game..86

Stating the Goal 96

Making a Plan..101

Seeing the Attempt 106

Introduction to the Story Problem

Objective

- Group the story grammar elements of *first event, response, goal, plan,* and *attempt* into the Problem category of a story

Preparing Materials

1. Duplicate *Story Grammar Puzzle* (page 75), one per student.

Preparing Students

We have learned about the setting of a story. We know that setting statements usually come at the beginning of a story, but they can also appear at other points of a story. We know that the Setting story grammar element includes the character, *the* place, *and the* time *of a story.*

[Take time to review the Setting components of *character, place,* and *time* as needed.]

Now we are next going to talk about a group of story grammar elements that make up the story Problem. Think back to the middle boxcar of the Story Train. This group of elements includes the first event, *the* response, *the* goal, *the* plan, *and the* attempt. *This group of story grammar elements deals with the problem or situation that occurs in the story and the attempt to solve it.*

Telling a good story is like putting a puzzle together. All the pieces need to be put together so that the story is complete, because a complete story is easier to understand and usually more interesting. We're going to practice learning the names of the story grammar elements that are included in the Problem of the story.

Activity Instructions

[Distribute one copy of *Story Grammar Puzzle* and a pen or pencil to each student.]

The Story Grammar Puzzle *on the page in front of you will be complete once you fill in the names of the story grammar elements that make up the Problem. Notice that the parts of the Setting—character, place, and time—are already filled in, since we have already learned about these. The* outcome *and* ending *pieces of the Solution part of the puzzle are also filled in, since we haven't learned about them yet. Notice that the Problem pieces of the puzzle have empty spaces. The words that fit into the puzzle pieces are listed at the bottom of the page. As I read about each of these story grammar elements, copy the name of the element*

Narrative Toolbox

you think I am describing into the correct piece of the puzzle. Once all the elements have been described, the Story Grammar Puzzle *will be complete. Listen carefully to each description.*

[Read through the names of the story grammar elements at the bottom of the page. Then read each of the following descriptions to students, pausing as necessary so that students have time to fill in the puzzle pieces. Help students locate the correct answers as needed.]

- *In space number 1, fill in the name of the story grammar element that refers to the first thing that happens in the story that triggers the main action of the story. This is the element that the main idea of the story starts from.* [first event]

- *In space number 2, fill in the name of the story grammar element that refers to how a character reacts to the first event of the story.* [response]

- *In space number 3, fill in the name of the story grammar element that refers to a character's idea for solving the main problem or situation of the story. This is what the character wants to happen.* [goal]

- *In space number 4, fill in the name of the story grammar element that refers to what a character will do to reach the goal.* [plan]

- *In space number 5, fill in the name of the story grammar element that refers to a character's actual actions for carrying out the plan.* [attempt]

[Take time to discuss the completed *Story Grammar Puzzle.*]

Finishing Thoughts

I want you to take your Story Grammar Puzzles *home. Point out each story grammar element on the page to a friend or family member. See how many of the elements you can describe. The next time you read or hear a story, see how many of the story grammar elements you can identify.*

Story Grammar Puzzle

Name: _____ Date: _____

Setting	Character
	Time
	Place
Problem	1. _____
	2. _____
	3. _____
	4. _____
	5. _____
Solution	Outcome
	Ending

First event	Response	Goal	Plan	Attempt

First Event Categories

Objective

- Identify the category (a change in nature or the environment; an action by another character; or a change in what the character hears, sees, feels, thinks, or remembers) to which the first event of a story belongs

Preparing Materials

1. Duplicate the three *First Event Posters* (pages 78–80). Enlarge, color, and mount them on poster board. If desired, laminate the posters for durability.

2. Gather a small flashlight; a beanbag; or a small, self-stick notepad for each student.

Preparing Students

Think about stories you know and movies you have seen. There is usually something that happens first that begins the main action of the story. For example, in the fairy tale Little Red Riding Hood, *the first event is that Little Red Riding Hood's grandmother is sick. This first event causes Little Red Riding Hood to travel to her grandmother's house to bring her food.*

[Discuss additional first events from popular stories or movies to help students become familiar with this concept.]

Remember the Story Grammar Puzzle *that we talked about? We learned that after we focus on the characters, place, and time that make up the setting of a story, we need to pay attention to the first event, which begins the problem in a story. The first event of a story may be one of three types, described in each of these posters.*

[Review and talk about each first event poster with students.]

- Type A *is a natural occurrence. This is when there is a change in the environment that is usually caused by nature or the weather. No one can control this type of occurrence from happening. Let's talk about some examples of this type of first event.*

[Provide time to talk about natural occurrences, such as a terrible storm, a girl's 5th birthday, or the death of a grandparent.]

- Type B *is an action by a character that causes another character to do something. Either the action by a character or what it causes another character to do could be the first event of a story.*

[Provide time to talk about character actions, such as being invited to a friend's sleepover, a teacher assigning a big science project, or a boy building a fort in his backyard.]

- Type C *is a change in a character. This may be a change in what the character hears, sees, feels, thinks, or remembers. This change can be the first event or can cause the first event.*

[Provide time to talk about character changes, such as someone deciding to do good deeds to help others, graduating from high school, or getting married.]

Let's hang these posters where all of us can see them.

Activity Instructions

[Distribute a flashlight, beanbag, or self-stick notepad to each student.]

Look at the First Event Posters. *I will be describing the first events of a variety of stories. Think about the first event as I talk about each one. Also think about the three different types of first events. I want you to shine your flashlight on (or throw your beanbag at, or stick a piece of note paper to) the poster that tells the type of first event I am describing.*

- *A peddler sold Jack some magical beans to plant.* [Type B]
- *Dorothy's house was torn out of the ground by a tornado and landed in Munchkin Land.* [Type A]
- *The wicked queen was furious when she heard that Snow White was more beautiful than she was.* [Type C]
- *During a terrible blizzard, the children became trapped in the mountains.* [Type A]
- *Lightning struck and started a fire that destroyed the town.* [Type A]
- *Tamara woke up crabby one morning, so she picked a fight with her friends.* [Type C]
- *The small kitten climbed the branches higher into the tree and became stuck.* [Type B]
- *Jack's brother broke Jack's new bike.* [Type B]
- *The girls in the fourth grade were mean to a new girl when she came to school.* [Type B]
- *Anthony finally remembered the combination to his locker.* [Type C]

Finishing Thoughts

When you go home tonight, tell a friend or family member what the first event of a story is. See if you can remember the three types of first events. Next time you read or listen to a story, think about what the first event is. See if you can decide what type of first event it is. And remember to make sure the first event is clear when you tell a story.

First Event Poster

TYPE A

A CHANGE IN NATURE OR THE ENVIRONMENT

First Event Poster

TYPE B

AN ACTION BY ANOTHER CHARACTER

First Event Poster

TYPE C

A CHANGE IN WHAT THE CHARACTER HEARS, SEES, FEELS, THINKS, OR REMEMBERS

First Event Scripts

Objective

- Retell a story starter that includes a setting description and one related first event statement

Preparing Materials

1. Duplicate *Story Scene—Jungle* and *Story Scene—Savanna* from Appendix J (pages 193 and 195). Color the two scenes and mount them on poster board. If desired, laminate the colored pictures for durability. The scenes for this activity should be appropriate for most students; if not, draw or locate alternate scenes.

2. Locate a Tarzan-like figurine for the jungle scene and a girl and a boy figurine for the savanna scene. Use figurines found at discount stores or garage sales, or use those provided in kids' meals from fast-food restaurants. If the precise figurine cannot be located, direct children to use their imaginations to pretend that a substitute figurine is a particular character. If scenes other than the jungle and the savanna are being used, locate appropriate figurines.

3. Duplicate *Story Starter Retelling Form—Jungle Scene* and *Story Starter Retelling Form—Savanna Scene* (pages 83–84), one per student. (Depending on time and interest, you may wish to have students use only one form.) Complete the Name and Date portions of the forms before meeting with students. If scenes other than those provided are being used, use *Story Starter Retelling Form—Blank* (page 85) to create a customized form.

Preparing Students

We have learned that a story needs to tell the setting, which explains who is in the story (characters), where the story occurs (place), and when the story takes place (time). We also know that a first event is needed to begin a story and we learned about the three types of first events. Let's try to remember the three types.

[Provide time to name and discuss the three types of first events: natural occurrence, character action, and character change.]

Activity Instructions

So that you can practice telling about the setting and the first event of a story, you will be looking at a scene while I tell the first part of a story. Then I will ask you to retell the story starter, making sure to tell about the setting and the first event. Listen closely as I tell about Tarzan in the jungle.

Narrative Toolbox

[Display *Story Scene—Jungle* for all to see. While using the Tarzan figurine, read the story starter provided in the shaded box on page 83.]

Now listen closely as I tell about Shandra and Eli in the savanna.

[Display *Story Scene—Savanna* for all to see. While using the girl and boy figurines, read the story starter provided in the shaded box on page 84.]

[Following each story starter, direct a student to retell the story. Using the appropriate *Story Starter Retelling Form,* transcribe the student's retelling. (Audiotape the student's retelling and transcribe at a later time, if desired.) On the form, also indicate the total number of sentences in the student's retelling and check (✓) the story components that were used. Provide each student with at least one turn to retell a story starter. Keep the completed *Story Starter Retelling Form*s in each student's file or portfolio. Repeat this task as needed to help students practice using detailed statements of setting and first event when starting a story. Review completed forms with students and save them in student files or portfolios.]

Finishing Thoughts

See if you can remember a story starter you learned today when you get home this evening. Try to tell the setting and first event to a friend or family member. You can even try to keep the story going by making up information to continue the story. Next time you read, hear, or tell a story, don't forget about the first event and how important it is to the rest of the story.

Story Starter Retelling Form— Jungle Scene

Name: _____   Date: _____

Tarzan was a young boy who lived in the jungle many years ago. Tarzan lived with a family of gorillas, so he wanted to be just like them. Tarzan wanted to play and swing from trees like the other gorillas. One day, Tarzan fell from a tall tree and hurt his legs very badly.

Student's Story Starter Retell:

_____

_____

_____

_____

_____

_____

_____

The retelling included _____ **sentences, including statements of:**

_____ **character(s)**   _____ **time**

_____ **place**   _____ **first event**

Story Starter Retelling Form—
Savanna Scene

Name: _____   Date: _____

> Shandra and Eli are a sister and brother who live in the savanna. One day while their parents went to town for groceries, Shandra was left in charge to watch Eli. While playing outside, Shandra lost track of Eli. He was nowhere to be found. The sun was going down and Shandra was getting frightened that she wouldn't find Eli.

Student's Story Starter Retell:

_____

_____

_____

_____

_____

_____

_____

_____

The retelling included _____ **sentences, including statements of:**

_____ **character(s)**   _____ **time**

_____ **place**   _____ **first event**

Story Starter Retelling Form—
Blank

Name: _____ Date: _____

Original Story Starter: _____

_____

_____

_____

_____

Student's Story Starter Retell:

_____

_____

_____

_____

_____

_____

_____

The retelling included _____ **sentences, including statements of:**

_____ **character(s)**   _____ **time**

_____ **place**   _____ **first event**

Response Card Game

Objectives

- Create a story starter using keyword prompts to include a character, place, time, and first event

- Complete a story starter by creating a response statement that goes along with the setting and first event

Preparing Materials

1. Duplicate *Character Cards, Place Cards, Time Cards,* and *First Event Cards* (pages 88–95). Copy each group of cards onto a different color of paper.

2. Cut the cards apart. Stack each type of card separately and set the four stacks in the middle of a playing surface.

Preparing Students

We have had lots of practice with the setting of stories. We know that the setting tells about the characters, the place, and the time. We just recently learned that the first event begins a story. We know that all of these need to be included to form an interesting beginning to a story. These items might also get mentioned, or may change, later in a story. Next we're going to learn about the response *story grammar element. The response tells about how a character feels or what a character does after the first event happens. Let's practice this idea. I have a list of first events that I will read. After I say each first event, let's think of a possible response.*

[Read each first event statement. Provide time for students to volunteer possible responses.]

- *Jessie drove her car into a snowbank.*
- *Fifi the poodle barked all night long.*
- *Jalen took $100 out of his bank account to buy toys.*
- *Dylan's mom saw him sneaking out of the house after dark.*

Activity Instructions

Now we're going to put all the story parts together that we have learned so far to start a story. You will notice four stacks of cards in front of us. One stack of cards contains the names of different story characters, one stack includes story places, one stack has story times, and one stack tells possible first events. [Tell the color of each stack as you name them.]

When it is your turn, take one card from each stack. Read each card and then put the cards in an order that makes sense to start a story. Practice saying the phrases so that it sounds like the beginning of a story. It may be a silly story. If the story starter doesn't sound quite right, you may need to change a word, like the action word, so that all the phrases go together. You will also need to think about a response that could go with your story starter. Practice saying your story starter in your head, being sure to make up a response statement at the end. Once everyone has had time to practice a story starter, you will each get a turn to say your story starter out loud.

[Provide time for students to choose their cards, organize their cards, and practice their story starters. Then have each student take a turn saying his or her story starter aloud to the entire group. Provide scaffolding cues and assistance as needed. If time permits, have students write their stories after they have had a chance to say them aloud to the group.]

Finishing Thoughts

Now you have learned 5 different story parts. When you are at home this evening, practice saying your story starter to a friend or family member. Try to complete your story with additional ideas. Remember to pay attention to the response to the first event in stories when you read, hear, or tell them.

Character Cards

my brother	the doctor
my dog	the principal
the prince	my family
a flying elephant	my dad

Character Cards

my friends	three evil monsters
a movie star	a dragon
a grizzly bear	my next-door neighbor
my teacher	my mom

Place Cards

at the mall	at my friend's house
in my classroom	in the hospital
at home	at the park
in a spaceship	at the store

Place Cards

in my backyard	at the pool
in my room	in the bathroom
in my neighborhood	in the lunchroom
on a bus	in the subway

Time Cards

before school	a billion years ago
during math class	10 minutes ago
five years ago	last winter
last night	next Monday

Time Cards

after school	long, long ago
next week	this morning
tomorrow	a while ago
right now	before supper

First Event Cards

read five books from cover to cover	crashed a bike into a parked car
wrote a letter and forgot to mail it	broke an arm
ate a whole package of cookies	scored the winning points in the big game
found an alien spaceship	grew over two inches in one week

First Event Cards

built a shed and forgot
to give it a door

found a suitcase
full of money

found a diamond ring
worth thousands of dollars

fell asleep in
some poison ivy

jumped out of a
burning building

started cleaning
everything in sight

tripped over a shoe

received a telephone call
from a movie star

Stating the Goal

Objective

- Identify and restate the goal of a story

Preparing Materials

1. Duplicate *Stating the Goal—1* and *Stating the Goal—2* (pages 98–99), one per student. (As another option, any story can be used with this activity. If a story other than the two provided is being used, duplicate *Stating the Goal—Blank* [page 100], one per student.)

Preparing Students

The next story grammar element that is included in the story Problem is the goal. *A goal is something someone wants to accomplish. Do you ever set goals in your life? Think of some of the goals that you have.*

[Provide time to talk about students' goals.]

In a story, the goal is set after the first event happens. The goal is a result of the first event. For example, if the first event in a story is that a man loses his dog, the goal might be to find the dog.

[Talk about additional first event and goal examples as needed to illustrate this concept.]

Today we're going to practice thinking about the goal *story grammar element by listening to a couple of short story starters and writing letters about the goals of the stories.*

Activity Instructions

[Distribute *Stating the Goal—1* and a pen or pencil to each student.]

On the top of this page, you'll see a short story starter. On the bottom of the page, you'll see space to write a short letter. The first thing you need to do is read the story starter. As you read, think about what the character's goal might be. Then pretend you are the main character in the story as you write a letter to a person of your choice, explaining the situation and telling your goal. If you need more room to write, use the back of the paper. Remember, your letter should mostly explain your goal.

[Provide students with time to complete *Stating the Goal—1*. Have students take turns reading their letters aloud, and take time to discuss the different versions of the letter. Then distribute *Stating the Goal—2* and conduct the activity once again. To make this process easier for students, you could read the stories aloud and have students dictate their letters into a tape recorder or to someone who can transcribe for them. As another option, have students write letters from the perspective of a character from any story, using *Stating the Goal—Blank* for the activity. Students should indicate on this page the name of the story, the name of the character, and the character's problem. Then students should write a letter from the perspective of the character, telling another person about the goal he or she has related to the problem.]

Finishing Thoughts

Now you can take your pages home and share the story starters and your letters with a friend or family member. Next time you read or listen to a story, pay attention to the goal that results from the first event. When you tell a story, be sure to state your goal so that your story is easy to understand.

Stating the Goal—1

Name: _____ Date: _____

1. Read the story starter below.

2. Pretend you are the main character in the story, and write a letter to someone who could help you with your goal. Describe your problem, tell how you feel, and explain your goal.

Story Starter

Marcus is an 11-year-old boy who lives with his mom and dad. Marcus's family was having a hard time since his father lost his job. Marcus had a great idea. One night, he asked his mom and dad, "Please, Mom and Dad, could I start a lawn-mowing business? I promise that I will do my homework and get good grades." Marcus's dad said, "No. That's too much work for you. I don't want to talk about it anymore." Marcus was disappointed. He knew that his dad was angry a lot since he had lost his job. His mom worked, but there still wasn't much money. That was the reason that Marcus wanted to start a lawn-mowing business. He could mow lawns on the weekends and after school. He wanted to earn some money to help his family.

Letter

Dear _____,

_____

_____

_____

_____

_____

_____

_____

Your Friend,

Marcus

Stating the Goal—2

Name: _____   Date: _____

Instructions

1. Read the story starter below.

2. Pretend you are the main character in the story, and write a letter to someone who could help you with your goal. Describe your problem, tell how you feel, and explain your goal.

Story Starter

Long ago, on a beautiful hill, there was a small wooden cottage. Inside the cottage lived a young woman named Mary. Next to the cottage was a large apple tree. Over the years, the tree had grown and grown until the branches formed a canopy over the roof of the cottage. Mary loved the tree and carefully took care of it. In the spring, the apple blossoms brightened the hillside. In the summer, the leaves from the tree kept the cottage cool. Mary used the apples to make sauces and pies. She used twigs and branches from the tree to start fires in the winter. One spring Mary noticed that insects were destroying the tree. The tree was starting to die. The branches were covered with the bugs. Mary wanted to save the tree!

Letter

Dear_____ **,**

_____

_____

_____

_____

_____

_____

_____

Your Friend,

Mary

Stating the Goal—Blank

Name: _____   Date: _____

Story Name: _____

Character Name: _____

Problem: _____

Letter

Dear _____,

_____

_____

_____

_____

_____

_____

Your Friend,

Making a Plan

Objective

- State a plan to help a character reach a goal

Preparing Materials

1. Duplicate *Making a Plan—1* and *Making a Plan—2* (pages 103–104), one per student. (As another option, any story can be used with this activity. If a story other than the two provided is being used, duplicate *Making a Plan—Blank* [page 105], one per student.)

Preparing Students

Today we need to remember back to the last time when we talked about the goal *story grammar element. We practiced looking at the goal by reading some story starters and pretending to be the main character in the story. Then we wrote letters to a friend to ask for help in reaching our goals. Today we are going to write letters again. This time we are going to write letters to the main characters of some stories to give them some advice. Let's talk about what* advice *means.*

[Provide time for students to discuss the meaning of *advice*. Help students see how advice can be related to making a plan to meet a goal.]

The letters you write today will give advice to the characters for a plan they might use to work toward their goals.

Activity Instructions

[Distribute one copy of *Making a Plan—1* and a pen or pencil to each student.]

On the top of this page, you'll see a story starter. On the bottom of the page, you'll see space to write a short letter. The first thing you need to do is read the story starter. As you read, you'll be able to figure out the problem and the character's goal. You should think about the advice you would give to the main character in the story for how to reach his or her goal. Then you should write a letter that explains your advice. Remember, if the main character chooses to follow your advice, this will become the plan to reach his or her goal. So be sure to give advice that could be turned into a real goal. If you need more room to write, use the back of the paper.

[Provide students with time to complete *Making a Plan—1*. Have students take turns reading their letters aloud, and take time to discuss the different versions of the letter. Then distribute *Making a*

Narrative Toolbox

Plan—2 and conduct the activity once again. To make this process easier for students, you could read the stories aloud and have students dictate their letters into a tape recorder or to someone who can transcribe for them. As another option, have students write advice letters to characters from any story, using *Making a Plan—Blank* for the activity. Students should indicate the name of the story, the name of the character, the character's problem, and the character's goal on this page. Then students should write a letter addressed to the character explaining a possible plan to achieve the stated goal.]

Finishing Thoughts

Now you can take your pages home and share them with a friend or family member. Explain how your advice can be changed into a plan for the character. When you read and listen to stories, try to figure out the plan that is being used to meet the goal. When you tell stories, be sure to explain plans the characters in the story are following to meet their goals. This will make your stories easier for everyone to understand.

Making a Plan—1

Name: _____ Date: _____

1. Read the story starter below.

2. Pretend you need to give advice to the main character in the story. Your advice will include a plan to meet the goal. Describe your plan by writing a letter to the character.

Story Starter

Marcus is an 11-year-old boy who lives with his mom and dad. Marcus's family was having a hard time since his father lost his job. Marcus had a great idea. One night, he asked his mom and dad, "Please, Mom and Dad, could I start a lawn-mowing business? I promise that I will do my homework and get good grades." Marcus's dad said, "No. That's too much work for you. I don't want to talk about it anymore." Marcus was disappointed. He knew that his dad was angry a lot since he had lost his job. His mom worked, but there still wasn't much money. That was the reason that Marcus wanted to start a lawn-mowing business. He could mow lawns on the weekends and after school. He wanted to earn some money to help his family.

Letter

Dear Marcus,

_____

_____

_____

_____

_____

Your Friend,

Making a Plan—2

Name: _____ Date: _____

Story Starter

Long ago, on a beautiful hill, there was a small wooden cottage. Inside the cottage lived a young woman named Mary. Next to the cottage was a large apple tree. Over the years, the tree had grown and grown until the branches formed a canopy over the roof of the cottage. Mary loved the tree and carefully took care of it. In the spring, the apple blossoms brightened the hillside. In the summer, the leaves from the tree kept the cottage cool. Mary used the apples to make sauces and pies. She used twigs and branches from the tree to start fires in the winter. One spring Mary noticed that insects were destroying the tree. The tree was starting to die. The branches were covered with the bugs. Mary wanted to save the tree!

Letter

Dear Mary,

_____

_____

_____

_____

_____

Your Friend,

Making a Plan—Blank

Name: _____ Date: _____

Instructions

1. Choose a main character from a story you know.
2. On the lines below, fill in the name of the story, the character's name, the character's problem, and the character's goal.
3. Pretend you need to give advice to the character. Your advice will include a plan to meet the goal. Describe your plan by writing a letter to the character.

Story Name: _____

Character Name: _____

Problem: _____

Goal: _____

Letter

Dear_____ ,

_____

_____

_____

_____

_____

_____

_____

Your Friend,

Seeing the Attempt

Objective

- Identify and evaluate a character's attempt to accomplish a goal

Preparing Materials

1. Duplicate *Making an Attempt—1* and *Making an Attempt—2* (pages 108–109), one per student.

Preparing Students

We have talked about the problem within a story. We know that the problem begins with the first event. Then there is the response, which is how the character reacts to the problem. Next we talked about the goal, which is what a character wants to have happen. What the character decides to do to accomplish the goal is the plan. The last story grammar element in the story Problem is the attempt. In the attempt, the character uses the plan to reach the goal. In some stories, a character's first attempt will be successful and he or she will reach the goal. In other stories, the character may need to attempt the plan more than one time to reach the goal or the plan may need to change as the story goes along.

To think about a character and his or her plan, think about the story Little Red Riding Hood. *Her plan was to take food to her grandmother, who was sick. To reach her goal, her attempt included walking through the woods alone and stopping to talk to a wolf along the way. What do you think about her attempt? Did it make it harder for her to reach her goal? Did she reach her goal anyway? What parts of the story helped* Little Red Riding Hood *with her attempt?*

[Provide time to discuss the story of *Little Red Riding Hood* and how the woodsman helped her attempt become successful.]

Activity Instructions

Today you will get a chance to read a couple of story starters. For each story, you will need to figure out the character's attempts and judge whether you think the attempts will be successful. If you don't think an attempt is going to be successful, you will need to recommend a better plan.

[Distribute one copy of *Making an Attempt—1* and a pen or pencil to each student. Provide students with time to complete the page. Discuss the students' responses. Then distribute *Making an Attempt—2* and conduct the activity once again. To make this process easier for students, read the stories aloud.]

Finishing Thoughts

I want you to take your completed pages home to share with a friend or family member. Explain what the word attempt *means to another person. When you are reading or listening to stories, think about the characters' attempts to use their plans. Think about why their attempts do or do not work for them. When you tell a story, be sure to make the character's attempt clear to your listeners. This will help them understand your stories better.*

Making an Attempt—1

Name: _____ Date: _____

Instructions

1. Read the story starter below.
2. Answer the questions that follow the story.

Story Starter

Shauna was so excited last week when she heard the news about the 6th grade science fair. She loved science and she really wanted to win first prize. The winners would receive a ribbon and have their pictures in the newspaper. While her science teacher suggested project ideas for the science fair, Shauna daydreamed about accepting the first-prize ribbon. When the information flyer about the science fair was handed out, Shauna lost hers, but she wasn't worried. She figured she'd find out the details some other time. The night before the science fair projects were due, Shauna decided to ask her mom and dad to help her think of a project idea.

What is Shauna's goal? _____

_____

What is Shauna's plan to reach the goal? _____

_____

Do you think that Shauna will be successful in reaching her goal? _____

Why or why not? _____

_____

_____

How could Shauna have changed her plan to make a better attempt? _____

_____

_____

Making an Attempt—2

Name: _____   Date: _____

Story Starter

Tim is a 10-year-old boy who loves music. Two months ago, Tim decided that he wanted to earn enough money to buy a stereo for his bedroom. Tim thought that it would be great to be able to go into his room and listen to a CD without his little brother bothering him. Tim decided to talk to his parents about ways he could earn money. Tim's parents said that he could earn extra money by doing special chores around the house. Tim and his parents made up a list of chores, like weeding the garden, washing the car, cleaning the garage, and sorting all the toys in the house. Tim started working on the list of chores right away.

What is Tim's goal? _____

_____

What is Tim's plan to reach the goal? _____

_____

Do you think that Tim will be successful in reaching his goal? _____

Why or why not? _____

_____

_____

What do you think will happen if Tim continues to do his special chores? _____

_____

_____

Story Solution

Outcome and Ending...113

Outcome and Ending

Objectives

- State a logical outcome of a given story
- Summarize a potential ending of a given story

Preparing Materials

1. Duplicate *Story Map—Math Class* and *Story Map—A Wild Ride* (pages 115–116), one per student. (As another option, consider using *Story Map 1 or Story Map 2* in Appendix H (pages 190–191) and filling in all the story grammar elements except *outcome* and *ending* using any appropriate story.)

Preparing Students

Let's review what we know about stories and story grammar elements. We know that a story needs to begin with the Setting, which tells us the characters, place, *and* time *of the story.*

Then as we go along in the story, we learn about the first event, *the* response, *the* goal, *the* plan, *and the* attempt *of the story. All five of those story grammar elements are grouped together as the Problem. The first event is the beginning of the problem. Then as the problem unfolds, we have a response, a goal, a plan, and an attempt.*

In the last part of the story, we find out about the outcome of the attempt, and then we hear the story's ending. The outcome *and the* ending *make up the Solution of the story. The outcome usually goes back to the first event of the story. In other words, the event that started the story is usually settled by the outcome. The outcome tells us how the plan worked and if the goal was met. The ending tells us how the story ends. A story may have a separate outcome and ending, or one sentence may tell both the outcome and the ending.*

To practice thinking about the outcome and ending, listen to these facts from some popular stories. See if you can guess the story that is being described in each example.

- *Outcome: When the glass slipper fit her foot, the prince took her to the palace and married her.*

   Ending: They lived happily ever after. [Cinderella]

- *Outcome: When the woodsman heard the cries of the little girl, he rushed to the cottage and frightened the wolf away.*

   Ending: They all sat down to enjoy fresh-baked goodies. [Little Red Riding Hood]

Narrative Toolbox

- *Outcome: The wolf fell down the chimney into a pot of boiling water.*

    Ending: The pigs all decided to live together in the sturdy house made of bricks. [The Three Little Pigs]

Activity Instructions

A story map shows all the story grammar elements of a complete story. We will be looking at some story maps that are missing their solutions. Remember that the Solution includes the outcome *and the* ending *of a story, so there will be two story grammar elements missing from each story map.*

[Distribute *Story Map—Math Class, Story Map—A Wild Ride,* and a pen or pencil to each student.]

Read through the information on each story map. Decide what the outcome and the ending could be for each story. Many different outcomes and endings could work for each story, but you must remember that the outcome should be related to the first event and should tell if the goal was met. Also, the ending should make sense based on the rest of the story.

[For students who need assistance with reading skills, read each story map aloud before having students complete the "Solution" section of each map. When students are finished with both maps, have them share their solutions with the group.]

Finishing Thoughts

Now you have learned about all the different story grammar elements. Take your Story Maps *home and read them to a friend or family member. When you are reading or listening to a story, think about how the outcome is related to the first event. Also, pay attention to the ending of the story. When you tell a story, make sure the outcome goes along with the first event in your story. If you include all the story grammar elements in your stories, people will have an easier time following your ideas and they will enjoy your stories even more!*

Story Map—Math Class

Name: _____ Date: _____

Setting

Character(s): my friend

Place: math class

Time: this morning

Problem

First Event: When my friend was taking a test in class, he noticed that the person next to him was copying his paper.

Response: He felt angry because he had studied for this test and he didn't want to be in trouble for cheating.

Goal: He wanted to teach the other person a lesson that cheating was wrong.

Plan: He decided to write the wrong answers on his paper and then switch them before the test was over.

Attempt: When he wrote down the answers on his test, he changed the numbers, so that if the answer was 54, he would write 45 instead.

Solution

Outcome: _____

_____

_____

Ending: _____

_____

_____

Story Map—A Wild Ride

Name: _____   Date: _____

Setting

Character(s): best friends, Carmen and Lee

Place: the amusement park

Time: last July

Problem

First Event: Carmen convinced Lee to spend a day at the amusement park, even though Lee was very afraid of the fast rides.

Response: Carmen was very excited. Lee was nervous.

Goal: Carmen was hoping Lee would ride the tallest, fastest roller coaster. Lee was hoping to ride only the slow rides.

Plan: Carmen convinced Lee to ride the tallest, fastest roller coaster by showing him how happy the people all looked as they got off the ride.

Attempt: Carmen and Lee got on the roller coaster. As it started up the tallest hill, the train stopped for a short moment.

Solution

Outcome: _____

_____

_____

Ending: _____

_____

_____

Solving the Story Puzzle

Retelling a Complete Story...119

Using Story Glue...126

Introducing a Story...133

Retelling a Story with a Complex Episode.......................................137

Stories with Multiple Episodes 144

Using Embedded Episodes 151

Retelling a Complete Story

Objective

- Retell a complete story, including story grammar elements: *setting (character, place, time), first event, response, goal, plan, attempt, outcome,* and *ending*

Preparing Materials

1. Duplicate *Story Scene—Jungle* and *Story Scene—Bedroom* from Appendix J (pages 193–194). Color the two scenes and mount them on poster board. If desired, laminate the colored pictures for durability. The scenes for this activity should be appropriate for most students; if not, draw or locate alternate scenes if desired.

2. Locate a Tarzan-like figurine for the jungle scene and a boy figurine for the bedroom scene. Use figurines found at discount stores or garage sales, or use those provided in kids' meals from fast-food restaurants. If the precise figurine cannot be located, direct children to use their imaginations to pretend that a substitute figurine is a particular character. If scenes other than the jungle and the bedroom are being used, locate appropriate figurines.

3. Duplicate *Story Retelling Form—Jungle* (page 121) and *Story Retelling Form—Bedroom* (page 123), one per student. (Depending on time and interest, you may wish to have students use only one form.) Complete the Name and Date portions of the forms before meeting with students. If scenes other than those provided are being used, use *Story Retelling Form—Blank* (page 125) to create a customized form.

4. Duplicate one copy of *Story Grammar Outline—Jungle* (page 122) and one copy of *Story Grammar Outline—Bedroom* (page 124). Consider enlarging these pages so that they are easier for all students to see.

Preparing Students

We have learned about all 8 story grammar elements in a complete story: the setting (including the characters, the place, and the time), the first event, the response, the goal, the plan, the attempt, the outcome, and the ending. Today you will get a chance to practice retelling a complete story including all of these story grammar elements.

Activity Instructions

Listen closely as I tell a story about Tarzan in the jungle.

[Display *Story Scene—Jungle* for all to see. Using the Tarzan figurine, tell the story in the shaded box on page 121.]

Narrative Toolbox

Now listen closely as I tell a story about Martin and his bedroom.

[Display the *Story Scene—Bedroom* for all to see. Using the boy figurine, tell the story in the shaded box on page 123.]

[Following each story, direct a student to retell the story in a similar way. Using *Story Retelling Form—Jungle* and *Story Retelling Form—Bedroom,* transcribe the student's story and check (✓) the story grammar elements that the student included in his or her retelling. (Audiotape the student's story and transcribe it at a later time, if desired.) Provide each student with at least one turn to retell a story. Discuss each student's retelling as a group. Talk about the story grammar elements that were included and those that were missed. Display and refer to *Story Grammar Outline—Jungle* and *Story Grammar Outline—Bedroom* while discussing these elements and the students' retellings. Keep completed *Story Retelling Form*s in student files or portfolios.]

[As an extension, conduct this activity having students tell original stories, rather than retelling the stories provided. Use *Story Retelling Form—Blank* to transcribe students' stories.]

Finishing Thoughts

Great job telling a complete story! There are many different story grammar elements to remember when telling or retelling a story. Now that you have retold these stories, try to tell one of them again to a friend or family member. Remember all 8 story grammar elements when you retell the story again. Keep all of these story grammar elements in mind whenever you read, hear, or tell a story.

Story Retelling Form—Jungle

Name: _____ Date: _____

Tarzan was a young boy who lived in the jungle many years ago. Tarzan lived with a family of gorillas, and he wanted to be just like them. Tarzan wanted to play and swing from trees like the other gorillas. He also wanted to grow hair all over his body, just like his gorilla family. One day, Tarzan had a terrific idea. He thought he could pretend to have hair all over his body if he covered himself with mud. So Tarzan went to the river and covered his face, his arms, his chest, and his legs with mud. He was completely covered and it almost looked like he had a brown, hairy body. Tarzan went to show the other gorillas. When they saw him, they laughed. Tarzan could not fool them. Tarzan felt sad and decided not to play with the gorillas the rest of the day.

Student's Retelling: (Continue on back of page if more room is needed.)

_____

_____

_____

_____

_____

_____

Check (✔) each story grammar element that was included in the student's retelling.

Setting   ___ character   ___ place   ___ time

Problem   ___ first event   ___ response   ___ goal   ___ plan   ___ attempt

Solution   ___ outcome   ___ ending

Story Grammar Outline—Jungle

Element	Story Facts
Setting	
character(s)	Tarzan; the gorillas
place	jungle
time	long ago
Problem	
first event	Tarzan wished he had hair all over his body like the gorillas.
response	Tarzan tried to think of a plan.
goal	Tarzan wanted to be like the gorillas and have a hairy body.
plan	He would pretend to have hair.
attempt	Tarzan went to the river and covered his body with mud.
Solution	
outcome	Tarzan was covered with mud, but the gorillas didn't believe it was hair. They laughed at Tarzan.
ending	Tarzan decided not to play with the gorillas the rest of the day.

Story Retelling Form—Bedroom

Name: _____ Date: _____

Martin is 12 years old, and he is finally going to have his own room. Martin's older brother, Diego, just moved away to college. Now Martin doesn't have to share a bedroom with Diego. Martin is so happy that he will have the room all to himself. Martin decides to make some changes in the room. He puts posters of his favorite baseball players on the walls, he moves the bed closer to the window, and he fills the two dresser drawers Diego used with his favorite snacks. After making these changes, Martin decides that the room looks great! To celebrate, Martin decides to invite friends over to spend the night, in his very own room!

Student's Retelling: (Continue on back of page if more room is needed.)

_____

_____

_____

_____

_____

_____

_____

Check (✔) each story grammar element that was included in the student's retelling.

Setting ___ character ___ place ___ time

Problem ___ first event ___ response ___ goal ___ plan ___ attempt

Solution ___ outcome ___ ending

Story Grammar Outline—Bedroom

Element	Story Facts
Setting	
character(s)	Martin; Diego
place	Martin's bedroom
time	present
Problem	
first event	Martin's brother Diego moves away to college.
response	Martin is so happy to have the bedroom to himself.
goal	Martin wants to make some changes in the bedroom.
plan	He would hang posters, move the bed, and use Diego's dresser drawers.
attempt	Martin made all the changes he planned.
Solution	
outcome	Martin thought the room was perfect.
ending	Martin invited some friends to sleep over to celebrate having his very own room.

Story Retelling Form—Blank

Name: _____ Date: _____

Student's Retelling: (Continue on back of page if more room is needed.)

_____

_____

_____

_____

_____

_____

_____

_____

_____

_____

_____

_____

_____

_____

Check (✔) each story grammar element that was included in the student's retelling.

Setting ___ character ___ place ___ time

Problem ___ first event ___ response ___ goal ___ plan ___ attempt

Solution ___ outcome ___ ending

Using Story Glue

Objective

- Use cohesive devices and transitional words to complete a narrative

Preparing Materials

1. Duplicate *Story Glue—The King's Story* (pages 128–129) and *Story Glue—T.J.'s Story* (pages 130–131), one per student.

2. Duplicate *Story Glue Words* (page 132), two per student.

Preparing Students

Have you ever put together a model from a kit? It may have been a car or an airplane. Maybe you have completed a craft project that had many pieces. Model kits and some craft projects come with many different parts. These parts need to be put together so that they make a complete project and so that they will not fall apart. What could be used to connect all the pieces?

[Provide time to discuss glue and its usefulness.]

In a story, we have words that work like glue because they hold the story together. Story Glue *means words such as first, then, next, after that, because, before, so, and finally. Story glue keeps a story moving and keeps it together. These words help the listener follow along, understand when a topic changes, and figure out the order of events in a story. Story glue words are very important to include in all the stories we tell and write.*

Activity Instructions

[Distribute *Story Glue—The King's Story,* one copy of *Story Glue Words,* a scissors, and some glue to each student.]

Look at this story. You will notice that many words are missing from the story. A story with missing words is not complete. The words that are missing from the story are story glue words. On the Story Glue Words *page, you will see many words to choose from that could be used to fill in the blanks in the story. Your job will be to glue the story together by filling in the story glue words of your choice. However, not all the words will make sense in all the blanks. You will need to choose words that make sense for each empty space. You will be able to figure out some appropriate word choices by finding out what happens in the story. I will read the story once before you get started, but I won't fill in any of the missing words. Follow along and start to think about the story glue words that might go best in each blank.*

[Read *Story Glue—The King's Story* aloud, leaving out the missing words. Help students read the list of words on *Story Glue Words.* Then direct students to cut out and glue on the story glue words where they belong in each blank space in the story. Then take time to read the story aloud again as a group, having students share their story glue responses along the way. Talk about how important the story glue words are to helping the story make sense. Following *The King's Story,* conduct the activity again using *Story Glue—T.J.'s Story* and the other page of *Story Glue Words.]*

Finishing Thoughts

You did an awesome job gluing those stories together! Now you can take your stories home and share them with a friend or family member. Explain what story glue words are to another person. Listen for story glue words the next time you read or hear a story and be sure to use story glue words the next time you tell a story. Your stories will surely be easier to follow and make more sense when you include these types of words!

Story Glue—The King's Story

Name: _____   Date: _____

1. Listen to the story.
2. Glue a story glue word that makes sense into each blank space of the story.

The King's Story

_____ upon a time there lived a king in a large castle. The king had

two daughters that he loved very much. The king knew that one day he would die

_____ one of his daughters would rule the country. He wanted to

choose the daughter who would lead the country with wisdom, fairness, and

kindness. _____ the king knew that both daughters wanted to become

the leader, the king decided to test his daughters.

One day, the king called his daughters to the castle. _____ the

oldest daughter, Eva, nervously entered the throne room. The king, smiled lovingly

at Eva. Eva knelt before her father. "Rise, my daughter," spoke the king. "I have one

question for you. Tell me, do you love your father?"

"Of course, Father," Eva replied. "I love you like I love the jewels in my crown." The

king nodded and kissed his daughter's cheek. _____ he dismissed her.

_____ his younger daughter, Ona, entered the throne room. Ona

glanced anxiously around the room. _____ she knelt, she knew that this

was an important moment. "Rise, my daughter," spoke the king. "I have only one

question for you to answer. Tell me, do you love your father?"

"Of course, Father," Ona answered. "I love you like I love the air I breathe."

_____ the king nodded and kissed his daughter's cheek.

_____ the king and his advisors met privately; the two girls waited

impatiently. They huddled together on a large sofa linking their hands together.

_____ many hours, the king called both girls back into the room.

"_____ we have reached a decision," announced the king. "With much

difficulty, we have chosen Ona to be the next leader. Jewels are pretty, but air is nec-

essary for life. Ona's wisdom will lead this country well. We have chosen Eva to be

the key advisor for her sister.

Both girls smiled at each other and hugged their father. _____ they

all lived happily ever after.

Story Glue—T.J.'s Story

Name: _____   Date: _____

T.J.'s Story

T.J. slammed the door and threw his helmet in the basket. "Hey," his mom called,

"What's all the noise for?"

"I am so sick of getting yelled at," T.J. replied. "All we did was skateboard in their

parking lot, and they made us leave. Where are we supposed to skateboard?"

T.J.'s mom rubbed his hair and said, "We'll talk about it after supper. Now go

wash your hands." _____ T.J. headed upstairs to wash.

_____ that night, T.J. called to his mom, "I have an idea," he shouted.

"Why can't we have a skate park in town? _____ we would have a

place to skate, and no one would yell at us."

His mom agreed that it was a great idea. "What do you think we can do?" she asked.

"_____ we'll get a sheet for people to sign their names," T.J. said.

"A petition," his mom stated.

"Right, _____ we'll ask some stores and restaurants to put a small box on the counter for people to put money in to help us _____ I'll call some of the guys to help too." T.J.'s mom smiled _____ T.J. raced to the phone. _____ T.J. called his friends, his mom made a list of things to do.

_____ collecting several pages of signatures, T.J. and his friends contacted other cities with skate parks. Their parents helped them put together a report that explained their plans and the costs.

_____ the big night arrived. The boys were dressed in their best clothes. They had to present their report, petitions, and donations to the city council.

_____ the meeting, the members of the city council listened carefully to the boys. _____ the council voted to study the report and discuss it at the _____ meeting.

T.J.'s mom hugged him and said, "I know that you are disappointed, _____ this is the way things happen. _____ T.J. and his friends had to wait _____ the next council meeting.

Story Glue Words

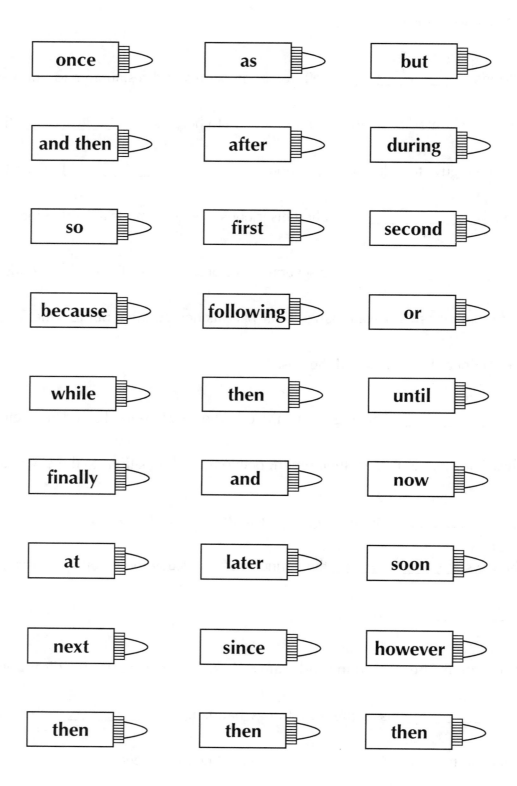

Introducing a Story

Objective

- Demonstrate how to introduce a story into a conversation

Preparing Materials

1. Duplicate *Story Introducers* (page 135) and cut the strips apart. Place the strips throughout the room or in a container.

2. Duplicate and enlarge one copy of *A Short Story* (page 136).

Preparing Students

We have learned all about 8 important story grammar elements. We have also learned how to put these pieces together to form a complete story. So now that you know how to tell a complete story, you will need to know how to introduce or begin a story when you are already talking with another person or with many people. We will be learning and practicing some special phrases that can help bridge a conversation to a story.

When we are talking with another person, we want to be skillful communicators. A skillful communicator is someone who is polite, stays on topic or changes topics appropriately, and is able to take turns in a conversation. Using a special phrase to introduce a story shows that you are polite, that you can stay on topic, and that you can change a topic appropriately. To show you some of these special phrases, let's play a quick game. I will say a phrase, and then you show me a thumbs-up if it sounds like a phrase that might be a polite way to introduce a story when you're having a conversation. Show me a thumbs-down if it does not sound like a good way to introduce a story. Here we go…

- *That reminds me of…*
- *I want to tell you about…*
- *Shut up so I can tell you something.*
- *Big deal! Listen to this…*
- *Like I care. I have a better story than that.*
- *In addition to that…*
- *When are you going to be done talking?*
- *Did I ever tell you about…?*
- *Something like that happened to me.*
- *You just made me think of…*
- *On that same idea…*
- *Along those same lines…*

Activity Instructions

[Set a copy of *A Short Story* where everyone can see it.]

Now you will get a chance to use a special phrase to introduce a story. I have placed some strips of paper around the room [or in this container]. Each strip of paper has a story introducer phrase on it. When it's your turn, I want you to find a strip of paper and read it to yourself. Then we'll start having a conversation. Sometime while we're talking, you need to use the story introducer and then start to tell a story. If you have a hard time thinking of a story to tell, you can tell this story that I have provided. [Refer to *A Short Story*.] You can also use a different story introducer than the one you choose. You just have to remember to introduce your story in a polite way. Your story either needs to be on the same topic that we're discussing, or you need to use a different type of special phrase to change the topic in an appropriate way.

[Provide time for each student to have at least one turn choosing a story introducer and introducing a story into an ongoing conversation.]

Finishing Thoughts

Take home the phrase you used to introduce a story today. Try to use this phrase or any others to remember to be a skillful communicator the next time you want to introduce a story into a conversation.

Story Introducers

Did you hear about...?

That reminds me of...

Did I ever tell you about...?

Something like that happened to me.

On that same idea...

That reminds me that I wanted to tell you about...

That makes me think of a story I heard.

In addition to that...

You just made me think of...

By the way, I wanted to tell you...

A Short Story

_____. Yesterday, my neighbor's

(Use a story introducer here.)

dog got loose. It was funny because the dog came over to our front door and wanted

to get in our house. Our cat started hissing and scratching at the door. Finally, my

neighbor caught his dog and took him home. It took my cat about an hour to calm

down after that.

Retelling a Story with a Complex Episode

Objective

- Retell a complex story that includes all 8 story grammar elements and more than one attempt

Preparing Materials

1. Duplicate *Story Scene—Bedroom* from Appendix J (page 194). Color the scene and mount it on poster board. If desired, laminate the colored picture for durability. The scene for this activity should be appropriate for most students; if not, draw or locate an alternate scene.

2. Locate a young boy figurine. Use figurines found at discount stores or garage sales, or use those provided in kids' meals from fast-food restaurants. If the precise figurine cannot be located, direct children to use their imaginations to pretend that a substitute figurine is a particular character. If a scene other than the bedroom is being used, locate an appropriate figurine.

3. Duplicate *Story Retelling Form—The Storm* (page 140) for each student. Complete the Name and Date portions of the form before meeting with students. If a scene other than that provided is being used, use *Story Retelling Form—Complex Episode* (page 141) to create a customized form.

4. Duplicate one copy of *Story Map—The Storm* (page 142). Consider enlarging this page so that it is easier for all students to see.

5. Duplicate *Multiple Attempts Story Map* (page 143), one per student.

Preparing Students

This morning, I had planned to wear my blue shirt with my blue pants to school. But when I went to my closet, I couldn't find the blue shirt. I looked all through the closet, but I couldn't find that shirt. I checked the laundry, but it wasn't there either. After searching for about 15 minutes, I finally found my shirt. It was missing a button, and it was in a pile of things to be mended. That meant that I had to find something else to wear today.

Sometimes, things don't work out the way we planned, so we have to think of something else. That happens in stories too. Characters may have a goal and a plan to meet that goal, but when they attempt it, something changes or gets in the way. That might mean that a character will need to make a different attempt, or it might mean that the character needs to change a goal or a plan. When a story has more than one plan, goal, or attempt, it is called a complex story.

Narrative Toolbox

Activity Instructions

[Display *Story Scene–Bedroom* for all to see. Tell the story *The Storm*, provided below, using a boy figurine.]

The Storm

Late one night, Jordan snuggled under the quilt on his bed while the rest of his family was asleep. The house made usual nighttime noises. The refrigerator in the kitchen hummed, the ceiling fan whirred, and the living room clock ticked. Unlike his brother, Jordan wasn't afraid of the dark. Actually, he enjoyed the quiet and the feeling that all of his family was sleeping peacefully.

When Jordan looked around his room, he saw a flash of light followed by a loud bang of thunder. Suddenly it happened again. Jordan couldn't even count the seconds after the lightning. The thunder was coming too fast. The wind was whipping against the windows, and the hard pellets of rain were bouncing off the roof. Jordan was wide awake now. He sat up in his bed with his eyes open in terror. This was a bad storm. The thunder, wind, and rain were scaring Jordan. Trying to block out the noise, he buried his head under the pillow. But that didn't work. He was still afraid.

Then, Jordan threw off the covers and ran into his dad's bedroom. He shook and shook his dad to awaken him, but Jordan's dad just rolled over and sighed.

Trudging back to his bedroom, Jordan spotted his headphones and boom box. He quickly looked through his tapes to find the loudest music he had. Jordan settled into bed with his headphones on and turned on the music. He closed his eyes tight and listened to the music until he fell asleep.

[Provide time for each student to retell the story *The Storm* using the scene and the figurine. Using *Story Retelling Form—The Storm*, transcribe each student's description. (Audiotape the student's story and transcribe it at a later time, if desired.) Discuss each student's performance following his or her retelling or during the next class time. On the form, check (✔) the story grammar elements that were used. If time permits, use *Story Map—The Storm* to recap the story grammar elements from the story. Have each student complete *Multiple Attempts Story Map* to map out their responses or the correct story grammar elements for *The Storm*, after everyone has had a chance to retell the story. Keep completed retelling forms in each student's file or portfolio.]

[Consider conducting this same type of activity again using model stories that have multiple goals or multiple plans. Create customized scenes, retelling forms, and story maps for these stories. Use figurines as appropriate.]

Finishing Thoughts

Now you've practiced telling stories that have some tricky situations. We know that all stories aren't simple, so we need to be good at telling and understanding stories that might have more than one goal, plan, or attempt. Practice telling these types of stories, and make sure your story grammar elements are clear. Take home your story map for The Storm *and tell this story to a friend or family member. When you are reading or listening to a story with more than one goal, plan, or attempt, follow along carefully so that you understand the action.*

Story Retelling Form—The Storm

Name: _____   Date: _____

Student's Retelling: (Continue on back of page if more room is needed.)

_____

_____

_____

_____

_____

_____

_____

_____

_____

_____

_____

_____

_____

_____

_____

_____

_____

Check (✓) each story grammar element that was included in the student's retelling. Place additional checks for multiple occurrences of each element.

Setting   ___ character   ___ place   ___ time

Problem   ___ first event   ___ response   ___ goal   ___ plan   ___ attempt

Solution   ___ outcome   ___ ending

Story Retelling Form—Complex Episode

Name: _____ Date: _____

Student's Retelling: (Continue on back of page if more room is needed.)

_____

_____

_____

_____

_____

_____

_____

_____

_____

_____

_____

_____

_____

_____

_____

_____

Check (✓) each story grammar element that was included in the student's retelling. Place additional checks for multiple occurrences of each element.

Setting   ___ character   ___ place   ___ time

Problem   ___ first event   ___ response   ___ goal   ___ plan   ___ attempt

Solution   ___ outcome   ___ ending

Story Map—The Storm

Element	Story Facts
Setting	
character(s)	Jordan; his dad
place	Jordan's house
time	late at night
Problem	
first event	A storm started.
response	Jordan was afraid.
goal	Jordan wanted to feel better.
plan	Jordan would block out the sound of the storm.
attempt 1	Jordan buried his head in his pillow.
attempt 2	Jordan tried to wake up his dad.
attempt 3	Jordan put his headphones on and listened to music.
Solution	
outcome	Jordan couldn't hear the storm.
ending	Jordan fell asleep.

Multiple Attempts Story Map

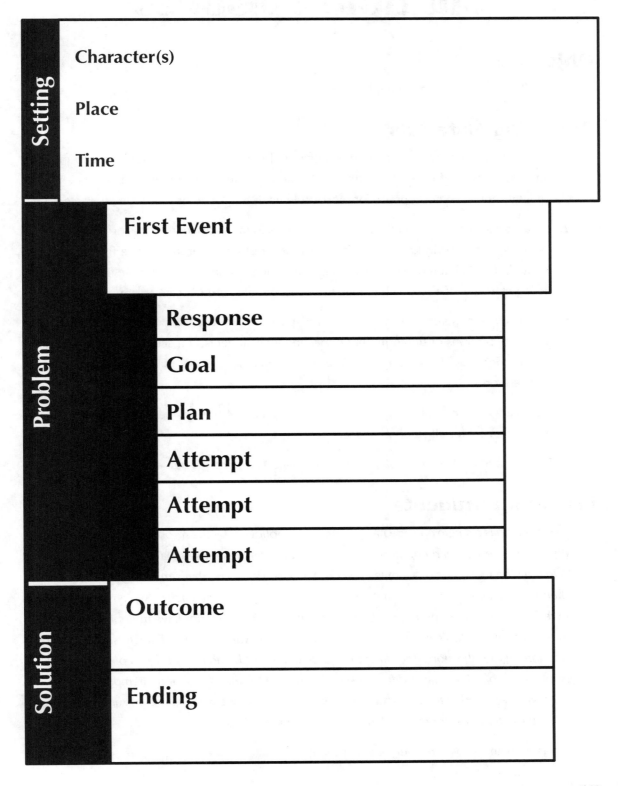

Stories with Multiple Episodes

Objective

- Retell a story containing multiple episodes

Preparing Materials

1. Duplicate *Story Scene—Jungle* from Appendix J (page 193). Color the scene and mount it on poster board. If desired, laminate the colored picture for durability. The scene for this activity should be appropriate for most students; if not, draw or locate an alternate scene.

2. Locate a soldier or woman figurine. Use figurines found at discount stores or garage sales, or use those provided in kids' meals from fast-food restaurants. If the precise figure cannot be located, direct children to use their imaginations to pretend that a substitute figurine is a particular character. If a scene other than the jungle is being used, locate an appropriate figurine.

3. Duplicate *Story Retelling Form—The Guard* (page 147) for each student. Complete the Name and Date portions of the form before meeting with students. If a scene other than that provided is being used, use *Story Retelling Form—Multiple Episodes* (page 148) to create a customized form.

4. Duplicate one copy of *Story Map—The Guard* (page 149). Consider enlarging this page so that it is easier for all students to see.

5. Duplicate *Story Map for Multiple Episodes* (page 150), one per student.

Preparing Students

A story that has a single episode has one first event followed by the response, goal, plan, and attempt. As we just learned, there can be more than one response, goal, plan, and attempt following the first event of a single episode. Many stories aren't that simple though. You will often read, hear, or tell a story that has more than one first event, each of which will be followed by a separate response, goal, plan, and attempt. These stories have multiple episodes. For stories with multiple episodes, you might be dealing with the same characters, place, and time throughout the story. The difference is that you will be able to find two or more main events, each of which has a different set of responses, goals, plans, and attempts. Then the story will be solved with an outcome and ending, just like we have learned. When we think about these types of stories, we can picture a diamond shape.

[Draw a large diamond where everyone can see it.]

Notice how the diamond is narrow at the top and at the bottom and wider through the middle. We can imagine the setting, *including character, place,* and *time, fitting in the narrow top part; many different episodes including their* first event, response, goal, plan, *and* attempt *elements across the middle; and the* outcome *and ending* elements *in the narrow part at the bottom. The story maps you'll be seeing for stories with multiple episodes will look like diamonds so that it is easier to picture these different episodes and how they are arranged.*

Activity Instructions

[Display the *Story Scene—Jungle* for all to see. Tell the story *The Guard,* provided below, using a soldier or woman figurine.]

The Guard

A young guard was sent far from her home to a remote post near the jungle. Her duty was to patrol the edge of the camp, watching for wild animals that strayed from the jungle.

One morning, the guard began her familiar patrol. She heard the chattering monkeys and the squawking birds. The moist, heavy air of the jungle settled around her. A cloud of insects surrounded her. As the sun rose higher in the sky, the guard began to tire. Her footsteps slowed while her eyelids drooped. The heat and boredom overwhelmed the young guard. "I need to rest a moment," she thought. She sat under a large tree, closed her eyes, and dropped her binoculars to the ground.

When the guard awoke, she quickly jumped to her feet. The sun was beginning to set. The guard realized that she had slept for a long time, so she reached for her binoculars to resume her patrol. But the binoculars were gone. Frantically, the guard searched the ground. "How could I have been so careless?" she asked herself. "I have to find those binoculars." The guard ventured into the thick brush of the jungle looking all around. She thought that the binocular strap must have caught on a branch. She pushed aside the heavy limbs and dense leaves that surrounded her.

Suddenly, the guard stopped and stared at a young gorilla in front of her holding the binoculars strap. The binoculars lay on the ground between the guard and the gorilla. The guard lunged forward and grabbed the binoculars, trying to pull the strap from the gorilla. As the guard rushed out of the jungle, tightly clutching the binoculars, the gorilla screamed angrily in protest. The guard knew that her carelessness could have allowed some of the animals to escape. From that moment on, the guard promised that she would never neglect her duty again.

Relieved that no animals had strayed while she was asleep, the guard continued her patrol.

Narrative Toolbox

[Provide time for each student to retell the story *The Guard* using the scene and the figurine. Using *Story Retelling Form—The Guard*, transcribe each student's description. (Audiotape the student's story and transcribe it at a later time, if desired.) On the form, check (✔) the story grammar elements that were used. Discuss each student's performance following his or her retelling or during the next class time. If time permits, use *Story Map—The Guard* to recap the story grammar elements from the story. After everyone has had a chance to retell the story, have each student complete *Story Map for Multiple Episodes* to map out their responses or the correct story grammar elements for *The Guard*. Keep completed retelling forms in each student's file or portfolio.]

[Consider conducting this same type of activity again using other model stories that have multiple episodes. Create customized scenes, retelling forms, and story maps for these stories. Use figurines as appropriate.]

Finishing Thoughts

Now you've practiced telling stories that have several first events. We can tell that these stories can be confusing, but they can also be very exciting and interesting to listen to. Since so much happens in our lives, many of the stories we tell might have multiple first events. Just remember to talk specifically about the responses, goals, plans, and attempts that follow each of the first events in the stories you tell. You might also find it helpful to follow along using Story Map for Multiple Episodes *when you read or listen to different stories.*

Story Retelling Form—The Guard

Name: _____ Date: _____

Student's Retelling: (Continue on back of page if more room is needed.)

_____

_____

_____

_____

_____

_____

_____

_____

_____

_____

_____

_____

_____

_____

Check (✔) each story grammar element that was included in the student's retelling. Place additional checks for multiple occurrences of each element.

Setting   ___ character   ___ place   ___ time

Problem   ___ first event   ___ response   ___ goal   ___ plan   ___ attempt

Solution   ___ outcome   ___ ending

Story Retelling Form–
Multiple Episodes

Name: _____ Date: _____

Student's Retelling: (Continue on back of page if more room is needed.)

_____

_____

_____

_____

_____

_____

_____

_____

_____

_____

_____

_____

_____

_____

_____

_____

Check (✔) each story grammar element that was included in the student's retelling. Place additional checks for multiple occurrences of each element.

Setting   ___ character   ___ place   ___ time

Problem   ___ first event   ___ response   ___ goal   ___ plan   ___ attempt

Solution   ___ outcome   ___ ending

Story Map—The Guard

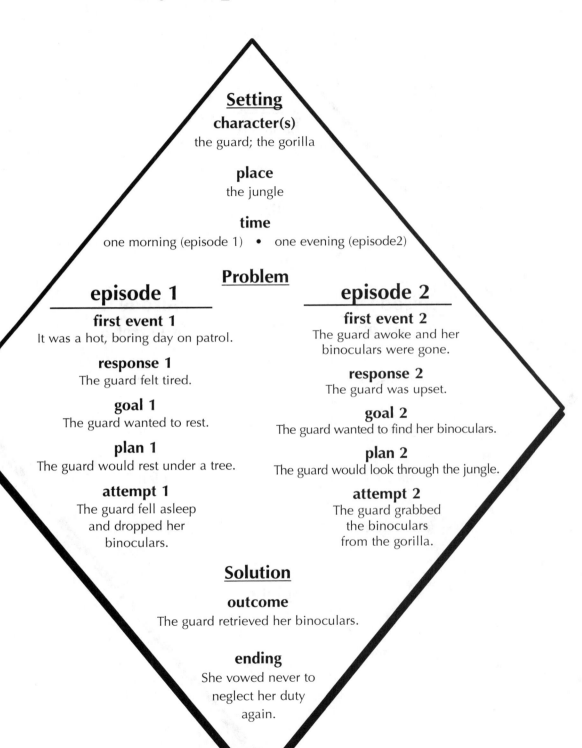

Setting

character(s)
the guard; the gorilla

place
the jungle

time
one morning (episode 1)   •   one evening (episode2)

Problem

episode 1

first event 1
It was a hot, boring day on patrol.

response 1
The guard felt tired.

goal 1
The guard wanted to rest.

plan 1
The guard would rest under a tree.

attempt 1
The guard fell asleep
and dropped her
binoculars.

episode 2

first event 2
The guard awoke and her
binoculars were gone.

response 2
The guard was upset.

goal 2
The guard wanted to find her binoculars.

plan 2
The guard would look through the jungle.

attempt 2
The guard grabbed
the binoculars
from the gorilla.

Solution

outcome
The guard retrieved her binoculars.

ending
She vowed never to
neglect her duty
again.

Story Map for Multiple Episodes

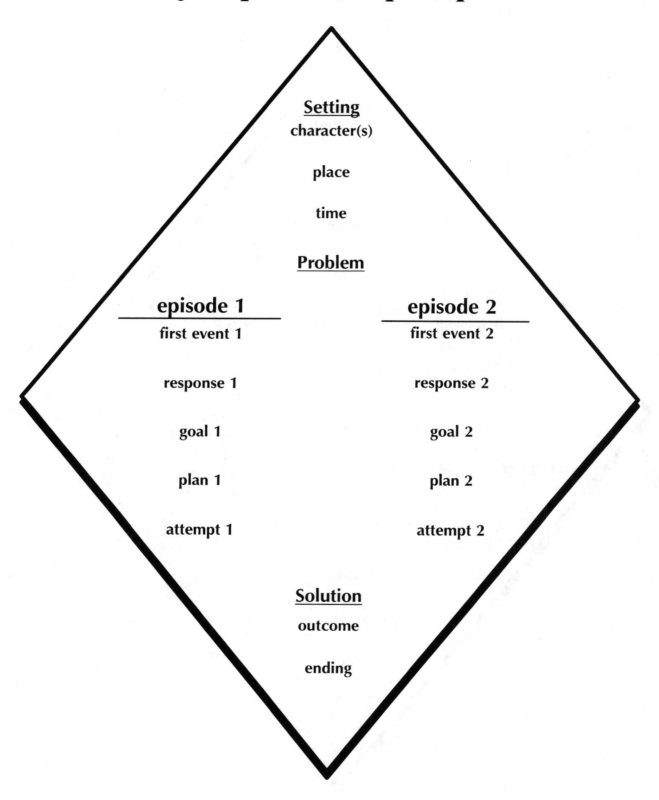

Setting

character(s)

place

time

Problem

episode 1	episode 2
first event 1	first event 2
response 1	response 2
goal 1	goal 2
plan 1	plan 2
attempt 1	attempt 2

Solution

outcome

ending

Using Embedded Episodes

Objective

- Retell a complete story that contains an embedded episode

Preparing Materials

1. Duplicate *Story Scene—Savanna* from Appendix J (page 195). Color the scene and mount it on poster board. If desired, laminate the colored picture scene for durability. The scene for this activity should be appropriate for most students; if not, draw or locate an alternate scene.

2. Locate a young girl figurine. Use figurines found at discount stores or garage sales, or use those provided in kids' meals from fast-food restaurants. If the precise figurine cannot be located, direct children to use their imaginations to pretend that a substitute figurine is a particular character. If a scene other than *Story Scene—Savanna* is being used, locate an appropriate figurine.

3. Duplicate *Story Retelling Form—The Sand* (page 154) for each student. Complete the Name and Date portions of the form before meeting with students. If a scene other than that provided is being used, use *Story Retelling Form—Embedded Episodes* (page 155) to create a customized form.

4. Duplicate one copy of *Story Map—The Sand* (page 156). Consider enlarging this page so that it is easier for all students to see.

5. Duplicate *Story Map for Embedded Episodes* (page 157), one per student.

Preparing Students

We know that stories can have two or more episodes. We've used a diamond shape to help us remember and place all of these different elements in stories that have multiple episodes. We've seen that these stories can be more exciting but sometimes trickier to follow. Now we're going to learn about and practice stories that have a shorter episode tucked inside the main episode. These stories have what are called embedded episodes. *It is also helpful to think of a diamond when we talk about a story with an embedded episode.*

[Draw a large diamond shape where everyone can see it. Label the following elements within the diamond.]

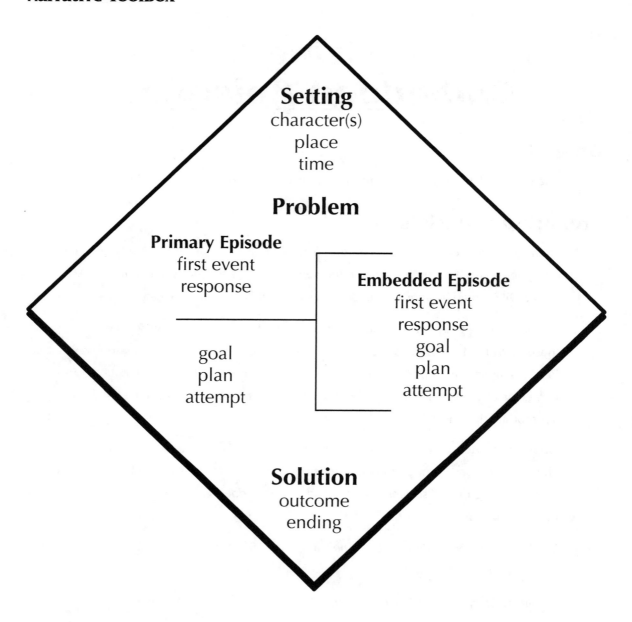

Notice that the main episode is called the *primary episode and the minor episode that inter-*
rupts the story is called the embedded episode. *Think of this diamond when we practice*
stories with embedded episodes.

Activity Instructions

[Display *Story Scene—Savanna* for all to see. Tell the story *The Sand* using a young girl figurine.]

The Sand

Neva waved to her grandfather as she headed out into the savanna. She was so excited because her grandfather had finally let her take a walk in the wild savanna alone. The warm sand felt good under Neva's feet, and the sun was shining brightly. She watched the beautiful trees and shiny rocks as she started to walk along.

As she walked, Neva saw a small shiny object peeking out from under a pile of sand. She stopped suddenly and started to head toward the shiny object to investigate. She bent down and quickly brushed the sand away from the object. Holding it up to her eyes, Neva caught her breath in surprise. It looked like a coin, but it wasn't a coin she had ever seen before. The writing on the coin was in a different language and the person on the coin was wearing old-fashioned clothing. Then Neva remembered a story her grandfather had once told her about how groups of nomads used to travel through the savanna with their treasures. The path Neva was on was the shortcut between two very important cities. Neva's grandfather had also said that many of the nomads would never reach their final destinations with all of their treasures. Strong storms would blow the bits of the treasures off the camel's backs. These precious gems and coins would then get buried in the savanna sand. Could this be a coin from an old treasure? Neva thought there might be more treasure buried nearby in the sand.

Neva fell to her hands and knees and started to dig through the sand. Before she found more treasure, Neva heard her grandfather call her name. It was time for her to return home. Quickly, Neva began running toward home. Her head was spinning about the buried treasures that could be waiting for her in the sand. As Neva got close to home, she noticed the worried look on her grandfather's face. She waved to him to reassure him that she was okay. When she waved, Neva realized her hands were empty. She must have dropped the coin while she was running. As she ran toward her grandfather, Neva tried to remember exactly what the coin looked like so she could describe it to him. She thought to herself, "I just have to find that coin again."

[Provide time for each student to retell the story of *The Sand* using the scene and the figurine. Using the *Story Retelling Form—The Sand,* transcribe each student's description. (Audiotape the student's story and transcribe it at a later time, if desired.) On the form, check (✔) the story grammar elements that were used.) Discuss each student's performance following his or her retelling or during the next class time. If time permits, use *Story Map—The Sand* to recap the story grammar elements from the story. After everyone has had a chance to retell the story, have each student complete *Story Map for Embedded Episodes* to map out their responses or the correct story grammar elements for *The Sand.* Keep completed retelling forms in student files or portfolios.]

Finishing Thoughts

Now you're an expert at telling stories. We've learned about all the story grammar elements and how they can combine to form complete stories and complex stories. We've had lots of practice telling many different stories. Remember to think about story grammar elements whenever you are listening to, reading, and telling stories. You are bound to understand a story better when you think about these elements. Also, you'll tell clearer and more exciting stories that your listener can understand when you consider all of these details.

Story Retelling Form—The Sand

Name: _____ Date: _____

Student's Retelling: (Continue on back of page if more room is needed.)

_____

_____

_____

_____

_____

_____

_____

_____

_____

_____

_____

_____

_____

_____

_____

_____

Check (✔) each story grammar element that was included in the student's retelling. Place additional checks for multiple occurrences of each element.

Setting ___ character ___ place ___ time

Problem ___ first event ___ response ___ goal ___ plan ___ attempt

Solution ___ outcome ___ ending

Story Retelling Form— Embedded Episodes

Name: _____ Date: _____

Student's Retelling: (Continue on back of page if more room is needed.)

_____

_____

_____

_____

_____

_____

_____

_____

_____

_____

_____

_____

_____

_____

_____

_____

_____

Check (✔) each story grammar element that was included in the student's retelling. Place additional checks for multiple occurrences of each element.

Setting ___ character ___ place ___ time

Problem ___ first event ___ response ___ goal ___ plan ___ attempt

Solution ___ outcome ___ ending

Story Map—The Sand

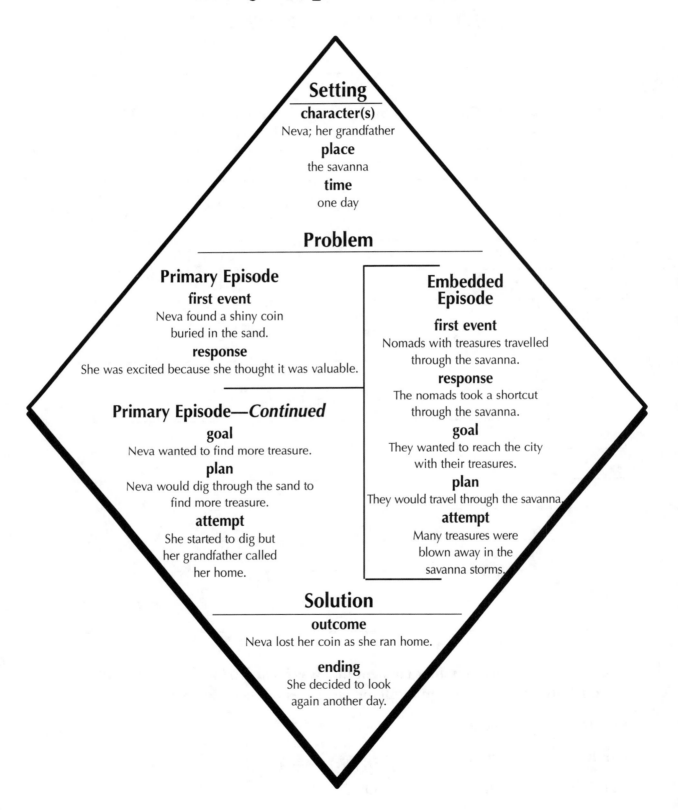

Setting

character(s)
Neva; her grandfather

place
the savanna

time
one day

Problem

Primary Episode

first event
Neva found a shiny coin
buried in the sand.

response
She was excited because she thought it was valuable.

Embedded Episode

first event
Nomads with treasures travelled
through the savanna.

response
The nomads took a shortcut
through the savanna.

goal
They wanted to reach the city
with their treasures.

plan
They would travel through the savanna.

attempt
Many treasures were
blown away in the
savanna storms.

Primary Episode—*Continued*

goal
Neva wanted to find more treasure.

plan
Neva would dig through the sand to
find more treasure.

attempt
She started to dig but
her grandfather called
her home.

Solution

outcome
Neva lost her coin as she ran home.

ending
She decided to look
again another day.

Story Map for Embedded Episodes

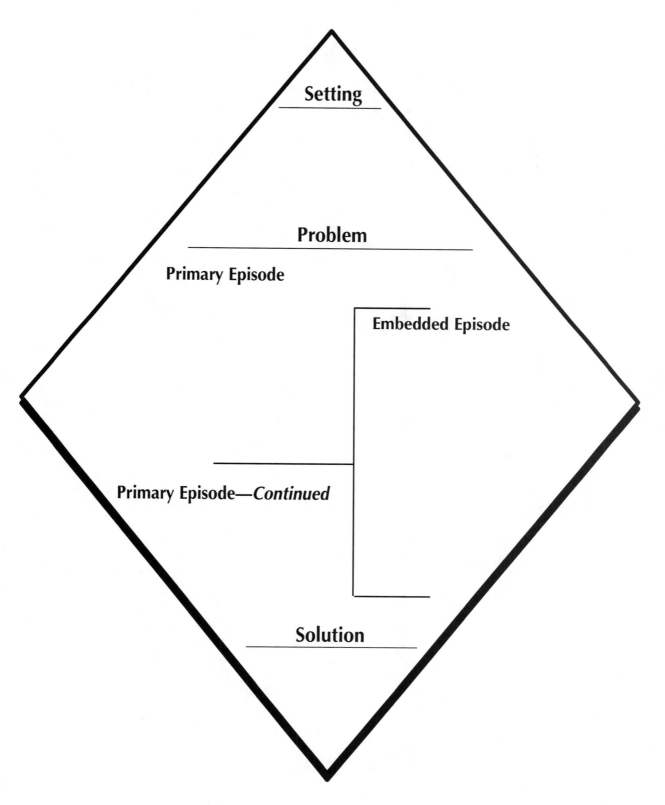

Setting

Problem

Primary Episode

Embedded Episode

Primary Episode—*Continued*

Solution

Written Narratives

Writing a Note 161

Writing a Story 167

Taking Messages 170

Writing a Note

Objective

- Retell a short story in the written form of a note including all essential story grammar elements

Preparing Materials

1. Duplicate *Bike Accident Note—1* or *Bike Accident Note—2* (pages 163–164) and *Soccer Game Note—1* or *Soccer Game Note—2* (pages 165–166), one per student. (Pages 163 and 165 provide more scaffolding and cues to help students complete a written note, while pages 164 and 166 simply provide the instructions and space for writing. Choose the best form to use with each student.)

Preparing Students

It's not only important to be able to understand stories and tell stories, it's also important to be able to write stories. Let's talk about all the different types of stories we can write.

[Provide time to discuss writing stories. Also discuss writing purposes such as journal writing, writing for class assignments, writing letters to friends, and writing notes to others.]

Wow! We can think of lots of times when it's important to know how to write a story. The stories we write might be quite long, like for a book report, or they might be short, like a note we would leave for a teacher. Writing notes are a great way to practice writing stories. These stories are usually short, but they might include all or some of the story grammar elements we've talked about.

Activity Instructions

Today you will all get a chance to write two different stories in the forms of notes. For each note, first you will listen to a short story and then you will write a note that tells about the story you heard. You will get to do this for two different stories. Be sure to listen carefully to each story.

[Distribute *Bike Accident Note—1* or *Bike Accident Note—2* and a pen or pencil to each student. Read the following story aloud.]

Narrative Toolbox

Bike Accident

You were riding your bike home from school. You swerved to miss a small pile of rocks on the sidewalk and your bike ran off the sidewalk. You fell off your bike. Your jacket ripped, the strap of your bookbag broke, and you got a bloody nose. You got back on your bike and made it home okay. You washed your hands and face, cleaned up your nose, and changed your clothes. You notice that your bike frame is bent a little and that the front tire feels a little wobbly. Now you have to leave to babysit at your cousin's house. Your parents will arrive home while you are gone, and they might notice your bent bike, your broken bookbag, your ripped jacket, and the blood on the shirt you just threw in with the laundry. You don't want them to worry, so you decide to leave them a note telling the story of what happened.

[Provide time for students to complete their *Bike Accident Note* pages. Help students as needed, to retell parts of the story.]

Now let's try this again with another short story and note.

[Distribute *Soccer Game Note—1* or *Soccer Game Note—2* to each student. Read the following story aloud.]

Soccer Game

The coach called you this morning after your parents left for work. He said that tonight's soccer game had been canceled because the other team has five players who are sick. The game will be played next Tuesday instead. Now your coach has scheduled practice for tonight. If it is raining, practice will be at the school gym. If it is sunny, practice will be at the city park field. You find out that you can get a ride to practice with your friend Sam, but you will need one of your parents to pick up you and Sam after practice at 5:30. You will be leaving for practice before either of your parents gets home from work, so you need to leave them a note explaining the situation and making sure that one of them picks you up after practice. Remember, Sam needs a ride home too!

[Provide time for students to complete their *Soccer Game Note* pages. Help students as needed, to retell parts of the story.]

Finishing Thoughts

We know how important it is to be able to explain a story in a note. Especially when another person will depend on the information in the note to do or understand something. Think about a story carefully the next time you write a note. Be sure to include all the important story grammar elements in your notes.

Bike Accident Note—1

Name: _____ Date: _____

1. Listen to the story about the bike accident.
2. Write a note to your parents explaining what happened. The phrases in the shaded box below might help you write your note.

My Note

Dear _____ ,

_____

_____

_____

_____

_____

_____

_____

Love,

bike frame is bent	babysitting	fell off my bike
riding my bike	bloody nose	hit the rocks
broken strap on bookbag	feel okay	this afternoon
coming home from school	got cleaned up	ripped my jacket

Bike Accident Note—2

Name: _____   Date: _____

1. Listen to the story about the bike accident.

2. Write a note to your parents explaining what happened.

My Note

Dear _____ ,

_____

_____

_____

_____

_____

_____

_____

_____

_____

Love,

Soccer Game Note—1

Name: _____ Date: _____

Instructions

1. Listen to the story about the soccer game.

2. Write a note to your parents explaining what happened. The phrases in the shaded box below might help you write your note.

My Note

Dear _____ ,

_____

_____

_____

_____

_____

_____

_____

_____

Love,

this morning	need a ride home	at 5:30
tonight's game is canceled	at the school gym	Sam needs a ride too
if it is raining	at the city park	the coach called
rescheduled for next Tuesday	if it is sunny	practice tonight instead

Soccer Game Note—2

Name: _____ Date: _____

My Note

Dear_____,

_____

_____

_____

_____

_____

_____

_____

_____

Love,

Writing a Story

Objective

- Write an original short story including all story grammar elements

Preparing Materials

1. Duplicate *Story Map—1* or *Story Map—2* from Appendix H (pages 190–191), one per student.

2. Duplicate one copy of *Fun Story Starters* (page 169). Cut the strips apart.

3. Duplicate one copy of *Story Glue Words* (page 132).

Preparing Students

We've had a little bit of practice writing a story in the form of a note. All of the details, or the story grammar elements, were given to us. It's also important to be able to make up a story, include all the story grammar elements, and write the story for others to read. It is so much fun to write stories! You can even add pictures to make your story come to life. Remember, when we write a story, just like when we tell stories and write notes, it's important to be clear about all the story grammar elements.

Activity Instructions

Today you will get a chance to make up and write a story for others to read. You will be using a copy of this Story Map *[hold up a copy of the selected* Story Map *from Appendix H] to help you think about including all the story grammar elements in your story. Before you start writing, you need to think about some of the main elements in your story. As you start to decide on some of these details, fill in the corresponding places on your* Story Map. *Once your* Story Map *is completed, you can write your story. And don't forget about those story glue words we practiced. I will have a sheet of* Story Glue Words *that you can look at when you start to write your story.*

[Distribute one copy of *Story Map—1* or *Story Map—2,* a pen or pencil, and one or more blank sheets of lined paper to each student. Have students choose a fun story starter strip if needed to help them get started with their stories. Keep a copy of *Story Glue Words* where everyone can see it. Help students complete their *Story Maps* and write their stories. Be sure all students' *Story Maps* are complete before having them go on to write their stories. Use scaffolding cues as necessary to help students complete their *Story Maps*. Have students dictate or word-process their stories if handwriting skills are insufficient. If time permits, or during a future class, have students illustrate their stories and/or read their stories aloud.]

Finishing Thoughts

Now that you have written a story of your own, take the story home to read to a friend or family member. Use special voices, emotions, and actions to tell your story if that makes it more fun. Remember all of these story grammar elements the next time you write a story in school or at home. Map out your story before you start writing. Count to make sure you have at least 8 story grammar elements written down; then you'll be sure to be on the right track to writing a great story!

Fun Story Starters

One sunny day, I was walking home from the park with
my sister and a dinosaur started to follow us.

Last spring, my teacher was sick one day and the
principal let me be the teacher for the day.

Last night, I was watching TV in the basement when all of the sudden
I heard extremely loud footsteps coming down the stairs.

As soon as I got home from school and unzipped my backpack,
I knew I had brought home the wrong book.

While I was riding the bus home from school, I opened the
book I had just checked out of the library and $100 fell into my lap.

While we were on a camping trip last summer, my friends and
I found a mysterious cave in the woods behind our camp.

Last Halloween, my brother and I dressed
up in the best costumes ever.

Believe it or not, it actually snowed on my birthday
last year; and my birthday is in June!

I had been feeling sick for several days when my dad finally made me go
to the doctor. To my surprise, my doctor was a 16-year-old girl!

The Martian creatures stepped off their spaceship.
They realized they must have landed on a planet they had never been to.

The pioneer cowboy and his family decided to move west to find farmland
and gold. They packed up their belongings and headed out in their wagon.

Taking Messages

Objective

- Write a telephone message including all the necessary information

Preparing Materials

1. Duplicate *Phone Call Log—1* and *Phone Call Log—2* (pages 173–174), one per student.

Preparing Students

Why do people leave messages when the person they want to talk with isn't available? Have you ever taken phone messages? How can we remember these messages even if we have to wait minutes or hours before we actually see the person who the message is for? What might happen if you forget a message or some details from a message? How is a telephone message like a short story? Let's see if we can answer some of these questions.

[Provide time to talk about telephone messages, how they are like short stories, and the importance of writing messages down.]

A telephone message is like a short story because there are certain elements that need to be a part of the message. Most telephone messages have characters, places, times, and first events. Some telephone messages even go on to describe a complete story that includes all the story grammar elements that we have discussed. When we take a telephone message, we need to include all the important information, such as who called and when he or she called. Listen to these telephone messages. Give me a thumbs-up if the telephone message sounds appropriate because all the information is included. Give me a thumbs-down if something is wrong with the telephone message because information is missing.

- *Mom, somebody called for you. I don't know who it was though.*

- *Mom, your meeting has been canceled for tonight. It will be tomorrow morning instead. Call Tyra at 924-6303 if you have any questions.*

- *Jenny, one of your friends called. I always forget her name. Sorry!*

- *Dad, that guy you work with called again. He said he'll be stopping over around 4:00. Or maybe it was 6:00. I can't remember.*

It's clear that we need to be careful about including all the important elements in the telephone messages that we take. We also know that it is best to write these messages down. It's not usually any easier to remember all the important details even as you get older. The most responsible thing to do when you take a telephone message is to get all the information written down so that the person receiving the message can understand it. Let's make a list of all the information we should include when we take a telephone message.

[Provide time to list and talk about details such as who the message is for, who called, when the call arrived, what the message is, if the other person will call back (and if so, when), and what his or her telephone number is.]

Activity Instructions

[Distribute *Phone Call Log—1, Phone Call Log—2,* and a pen or pencil to each student.]

Now you will get a chance to practice writing short stories as you take a variety of telephone messages. I will pretend to be the person calling, and you will be the person taking the message. First listen to my message. Then write the message using any of the spaces on the forms. As you are writing the message, feel free to raise your hand and ask additional questions that might help you make your message complete. Asking questions is a great strategy to use when taking a telephone message.

[Read each of the following telephone messages. After each message, provide time for students to write their notes on their log pages. Answer students' questions as they are asked. When students are finished writing each message, move on to the next. When all messages have been used, have students share their messages to check for accuracy. Talk about details that were extraneous and/or omitted.]

- *Please ask your mother to call Maddie tomorrow morning at work. The number is 723-6210. Thank you.*

- *Yes, this is John from the post office calling. We have a package for Tony that won't fit in the mailbox. Please call 888-8885 to make arrangements for delivery of the package.*

- *Hi, this is your wonderful big sister, Grace. Tell Dad to pick me up at the video store at 7:30 not 7:00. Don't forget to tell him. Oh, and ask him to pick me up on the Oak Street side this time, not on Main Street. Thanks!*

- *Hi, this is George from the Many Miles Repair Shop. Tell your parents that their car is finished and ready to be picked up. We close at 5:00 Monday through Friday and at noon on Saturday. Oh, please tell them that the final bill comes to $327. Have them call 595-9999 if they have any questions.*

- *Could you have your Dad call Lee at home tonight? The number is 297-8287. Tell him it's not an emergency, but I would like to talk to him this evening. It's about the meeting tomorrow. Thanks.*

Finishing Thoughts

You will find that you will take many telephone messages during your life. People will see you as a responsible person and a skillful communicator if you write these messages down carefully. Practice taking telephone messages by playing a game of Telephone with a friend or family member. You can take turns giving each other messages and taking messages. Remember to think of telephone messages as little stories. Don't forget any of the important story grammar elements in the messages you take.

Phone Call Log—1

Name: _____ Date: _____

1. Listen carefully to each telephone message.

2. Write each message in one of the spaces provided.

Phone Call Log—2

Name: _____ Date: _____

1. Listen carefully to each telephone message.

2. Write each message in one of the spaces provided.

Appendices

Appendix A: Narrative Levels Analysis Form 177

Appendix B: Retelling Rubrics 178

Appendix C: Story Creation Rubrics 180

Appendix D: Story Rating Scale 182

Appendix E: Recommended Children's Literature 183

Appendix F: Strategies for Reading Stories Aloud 186

Appendix G: Scaffolding Questions...187

Appendix H: Story Maps 190

Appendix I: Feedback Form...192

Appendix J: Story Scenes..193

Narrative Levels Analysis Form

Name: _____   Date: _____

Age: _____   Teacher: _____

Place check marks (✓) to reflect the highest level of narrative development for formulated and reformulated tasks.

Description of formulated task: _____

_____

Description of reformulated task: _____

_____

Cognitive Stage	Approximate Age of Emergence	Mode	Formulated	Reformulated
Pre-operational	2 years	Heaps		
	2–3 years	Sequences		
	3–4 years	Primitive Narratives		
	4–4½ years	Unfocused Chains		
	5 years	Focused Chains		
	6–7 years	True Narratives		
Concrete	7–11 years	Narrative Summaries		
	11–12 years	Complex Narratives		
Formal	13–15 years	Analysis		
	16 years to adult	Generalization		

Comments:

Retelling Rubric—1

Name: _____ Date: _____

Age: _____ Teacher: _____

Title of Story: _____

Names all main characters Tells all major events Uses an accurate sequence of events Tells a favorite part of the story Needs one or no prompts	**5**
Names all main characters Tells all major events Tells a favorite part of the story Needs one prompt	**4**
Names all main characters Tells at least two main events Tells a favorite part of the story Needs two prompts	**3**
Names at least one main character Tells at least one main event Tells a favorite part of the story Needs two prompts	**2**
Names a character or an event Tells a favorite part of the story Needs more than two prompts	**1**

From *Literacy as a Key Element of Our Speech and Language Interventions,* by J. Montgomery, (1998, July). Paper presented at the American Speech-Language-Hearing Association's Achieving Successful Outcomes in Schools convention, Chicago, IL. © 1998 by J. Montgomery. Adapted with permission.

Retelling Rubric—2

Name: _____ Date: _____

Age: _____ Teacher: _____

Title of Story: _____

Begins with an introduction Names all main characters Tells the time and place Identifies the first event Tells a response	Names a specific goal States a plan Tells about the outcome and ending Needs one or no prompts

5

Begins with an introduction Names all main characters Tells the time and place Identifies the first event	Names a specific goal States a plan Tells about the outcome and ending Needs one prompt

4

Names all main characters
Tells the time and place
Names a specific goal
Tells a partial plan
Tells about the outcome and ending
Needs two prompts

3

Names all main characters
Tells the time or place
Tells the goal or a partial plan
Tells about the outcome or ending
Needs two prompts

2

Names some characters
Tells the goal or partial plan
Tells about the outcome or ending
Needs two prompts

1

Story Creation Rubric—1

Name: _____ Date: _____

Age: _____ Teacher: _____

Title of Story: _____

Begins with "Once upon a time…" or another suitable introduction Introduces characters Gives time and place information Sequences two or more events States feelings of one or more characters Has an outcome and ending Needs one or no prompts	**5**
Begins with "Once upon a time…" or another suitable introduction Introduces main characters Gives time or place Gives two events States feelings of one or more characters Has an outcome or ending Needs one prompt	**4**
Introduces main characters Gives time or place Gives two events States feelings of one or more characters Has an outcome or ending Needs two prompts	**3**
Introduces main characters Gives two events States feelings of one or more characters Has an outcome or ending Needs two prompts	**2**
Introduces main characters Gives an event Has an outcome or ending Needs two prompts	**1**

Story Creation Rubric—2

Name: _____ Date: _____

Age: _____ Teacher: _____

Title of Story: _____

Introduces characters
Gives time and place information
Identifies the first event
Details response to first event
Expresses a goal
Details plan and/or attempt
	Verbalizes the feelings of at least
	   one character
	Describes the outcome and ending
	Makes a concluding remark such as
	   a moral, lesson, or opinion
	Needs one or no prompts
		5

Introduces main characters
Gives time or place information
Identifies first event
Expresses goal and/or plan to reach
   the goal
	Sequences two or more events
	Verbalizes feelings of at least one
	   character
	Describes an outcome or ending
	Needs one prompt
		4

Introduces main characters
Gives time or place information
Identifies first event and/or
   the response
Expresses goal and/or plan to
   reach the goal
	Sequences two or more events
	Describes an outcome or ending
	Needs two or more prompts
		3

Introduces main characters Gives time and/or place Expresses the goal	States two or more events Describes an outcome or ending Needs two or more prompts	**2**
Introduces main characters Gives time and/or place Gives an event States an outcome or ending Needs two or more prompts		**1**

Story Rating Scale

Name: _____   Date: _____

Age: _____   Teacher: _____

Title of Story: _____

Check one: _____ Story Retelling Task   _____ Story Creation Task

Scale			
0 (Not at all)	1 (Suggestion of use)	2 (Weak inclusion)	3 (Clearly included)

Objective	Rating			
Includes setting character statements	0	1	2	3
Includes setting place statements	0	1	2	3
Includes setting time statements	0	1	2	3
Includes statement of first event	0	1	2	3
Includes response to first event	0	1	2	3
States at least one goal	0	1	2	3
Describes a plan to reach the goal	0	1	2	3
Explains the attempt	0	1	2	3
States the outcome	0	1	2	3
Provides an ending	0	1	2	3
Uses complete sentences	0	1	2	3
Uses transitional words to connect statements	0	1	2	3
Sequences events accurately	0	1	2	3
Uses appropriate grammar	0	1	2	3
Uses a variety of vocabulary	0	1	2	3

Comments:

Recommended Children's Literature

Alexander and the Terrible, Horrible, No Good, Very Bad Day (1987)
by Judith Viorst, illustrated by Ray Cruz
New York: Aladdin

Amelia Bedelia (2000)
by Peggy Parish
New York: Lectorum

Beats Me, Claude (1986)
by Joan Nixon
New York: Viking

Big, Bad Bruce (1982)
by Bill Peet
Boston: Houghton Mifflin

The Blossoms and the Green Phantom (1988)
by Betsy Cromer Byars
New York: Delacorte

The Blossoms Meet the Vulture Lady (1986)
by Betsy Cromer Byars
New York: Yearling Books

Bunnicula: A Rabbit-Tale of Mystery (2000)
by Deborah and James Howe
New York: Aladdin

Caps for Sale (1987)
by Esphyr Slobodkina
New York: HarperTrophy

Carl Goes to Daycare (1995)
by Alexandra Day
New York: Farrar, Straus and Giroux

Carl Goes Shopping (1992)
by Alexandra Day
New York: Farrar, Straus and Giroux

Carl's Afternoon in the Park (1992)
by Alexandra Day
New York: Farrar, Straus and Giroux

The Celery Stalks at Midnight (1989)
by James Howe
New York: Avon

Dear Mr. Henshaw (2000)
by Beverly Cleary
New York: Camelot

Freckle Juice (1995)
by Judy Blume
New York: Houghton Mifflin

Good Dog, Carl (1997)
by Alexandra Day
New York: Aladdin

Home for a Dinosaur (1992)
by Eileen Curran
Mahwah, NJ: Troll

Howliday Inn (1996)
by James Howe
New York: Avon

Ida Early Comes Over the Mountain (1990)
by Robert Burch
New York: Puffin

Narrative Toolbox

If You Give a Mouse a Cookie (2000)
by Laura Joffe Numeroff
New York: HarperFestival

In the Dinosaur's Paw (1985)
by Patricia Reilly Giff
New York: Yearling Books

Ira Sleeps Over (1975)
by Bernard Waber
New York: Houghton Mifflin

Kevin Corbett Eats Flies (1989)
by Patricia Hermes
New York: Minstrel Books

The Knight and the Dragon (1998)
by Tomie DePaola
New York: Paper Star

Let's Go Home, Little Bear (1995)
by Martin Waddell
Cambridge, MA: Candlewick Press

Milk and Cookies (1982)
by Frank Asch
New York: Parents Magazine Press

The Mitten: A Ukrainian Folk Tale (1989)
adapted by Jan Brett
New York: Putnam

Mufaro's Beautiful Daughters: An African Tale
(1987)
by John Steptoe, translated by Clarita Kohen
New York: Lothrop, Lee, and Shepard Books

My Side of the Mountain (2000)
by Jean Craighead George
New York: Penguin

The Not-Just-Anybody Family (1987)
by Betsy Cromer Byars
New York: Yearling Books

Obadiah (1990)
by J. Melser and J. Cowley
Bothell, WA: The Wright Group

Oliver Dibbs and the Dinosaur Cause (1986)
by Barbara Steiner
New York: Avon Books

The Pain and the Great One (1985)
by Judy Blume
New York: Dell

The Paper Bag Princess (1988)
by Robert N. Munsch
Toronto: Annick Press

The Puppy Who Wanted a Boy (1988)
by Jane Thayer
New York: Morrow

The Rainbow Fish (1996)
by Marcus Pfister
New York: North-South Books

Ramona Quimby, Age 8 (1992)
by Beverly Cleary
New York: Camelot

Rocking Horse Christmas (1997)
by Mary Pope Osborne
New York: Scholastic

Sarah, Plain and Tall (1987)
by Patricia MacLachlan
New York: HarperTrophy

The Snowman (1989)
by Raymond Briggs
New York: Random House

Sounder (1989)
by William H. Armstrong
New York: HarperCollins

Stellaluna (1993)
by Janell Cannon
San Diego, CA: Harcourt Brace

Tales of a Fourth Grade Nothing (1976)
by Judy Blume
New York: Yearling Books

This Island Isn't Big Enough for the Four of Us
 (1989)
by Gery Greer and Bob Ruddick
New York: HarperTrophy

Through the Hidden Door (1989)
by Rosemary Wells
New York: Scholastic

Tuck Everlasting (2000)
by Natalie Babbitt
New York: Sunburst

Two Good Friends (1974)
by Judy Delton
New York: Crown

Who Is the Beast? (1994)
by Keith Baker
San Diego, CA: Voyager

Strategies for Reading Stories Aloud

Prior to reading to children:

- Discuss the title, author, and illustrations
- Discuss the topic of the story
- Establish a purpose for the reading task

While reading to children:

- Stop and summarize events frequently
- Predict what will happen next
- Focus students' attention on new vocabulary

After reading to children:

- Reflect on the story events and characters
- Discuss lessons learned
- Link the story and characters to other books or topics

Scaffolding Questions

For children currently using:

Heaps • Sequences

Primitive narratives • Unfocused chains

Types of scaffolding questions to use:

Who are the main characters in the story?

Where does the story take place?

When does the story take place?

What happens in the story?

Who does (<u>event</u>)?

How does (<u>event</u>) happen?

How does (<u>character</u>) do (<u>event</u>)?

What happens after, before,
or as (<u>event</u>) is taking place?

Scaffolding Questions

For children currently using:

Focused chains

True narratives

Types of scaffolding questions to use:

What does (character) think, feel, or do about (event or character)?

From the clues in the story, what can you tell me about (the time)?

What does the author mean with these words: (phrase)?

(Character) said (dialogue) in the story. What is another way to say the same thing?

Why do you think (character) did (event)?

Why do you think (event) happened?

Why do you think the author/you chose this setting?

Why do you think the author/you chose this ending?

Who is the main character in the story?

What is the goal in the story?

How is the goal attempted?

What are the main events in the story?

In as few words as possible, tell what the story is about.

Did you like the story? Why or why not?

How could the story be improved?

Would you read other books by this author?

Would you recommend this book to your friends?

Was the author stating fact or opinion?

Scaffolding Questions

For children currently using:

Summarization

Complex

Types of scaffolding questions to use:

Was the author trying to develop a special lesson in the story? What is it?

What can we learn from (<u>character</u>)?

What can we learn from (<u>specific event[s]</u>)?

What was the theme of the story?

(<u>Character</u>) felt (<u>feeling</u>) when (<u>event</u>). Have you ever felt that way?

(<u>Character</u>) reacted to (<u>event</u> or <u>character</u>) by (<u>reaction</u>). How would you have reacted? Could (<u>character</u>) have handled the situation better?

Here is a new situation that (<u>character</u>) is in: (<u>create a new event</u>). Knowing what you do about this character, how will he or she react?

Create a new ending for the story.

Create a new setting for the story.

Create a new time for the story.

Add a new character/yourself to the story. How would the story change?

Can you think of another story that has a similar setting?

Can you think of another story that takes place during the same time period?

Can you think of another story that has similar characters?

Can you think of another story that has a similar plot?

Story Map—1

Setting

Character(s)

Place

Time

Problem

First Event

Response

Goal

Plan

Attempt

Solution

Outcome

Ending

Story Map—2

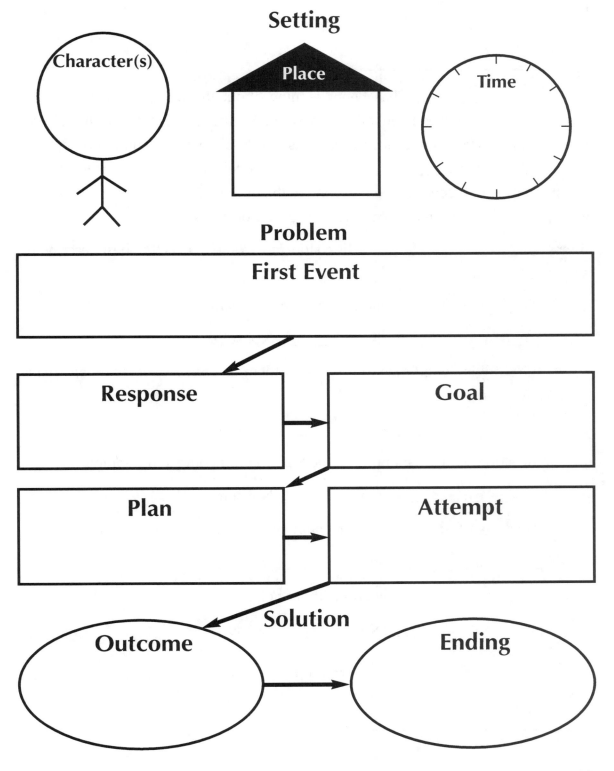

Setting

Character(s)

Place

Time

Problem

First Event

Response

Goal

Plan

Attempt

Solution

Outcome

Ending

Feedback Form

Date _____

Dear _____ ,

_____ has been learning about the parts, or elements, of a complete story. We have been talking about the Setting, which includes the *characters, time,* and *place* of the story, as well as the Problem and Solution components of a story. Please ask _____ to tell you a story or relate an event that has happened recently. Then respond to the questions that follow and return this form to me. This will help me monitor his or her progress.

After _____ tells a story, check the blanks that best describe his or her performance.

1. The story included mention of the Setting *(characters, place,* and *time).*

   _____ Yes   _____ No   _____ Not sure

2. The story included mention of the Problem *(events, responses, goals, plans,* and *attempts).*

   _____ Yes   _____ No   _____ Not sure

3. The story included mention of the Solution *(outcome* and *ending).*

   _____ Yes   _____ No   _____ Not sure

4. Words like *first, next, then,* or *finally* were used in the story.

   _____ Yes   _____ No   _____ Not sure

5. The story was told easily and without help.

   _____ Yes   _____ No   _____ Not sure

Thank you for your help. Please return this form to me by _____.

_____
(Sign)

Story Scene—Jungle

Story Scene—Bedroom

Story Scene—Savanna

References

Applebee, A. (1978). *The child's concept of story.* Chicago: University of Chicago Press.

Applebee, A., and Langer, J. (1983). Instructional scaffolding: Reading and writing as natural language activities. *Language Arts, 60*(2), 168–175.

Ault, R. (1977). *Children's cognitive development.* New York: Oxford University Press.

Coleman, N. (1997). *Step-by-step narratives: Illustrated lessons for telling and writing stories.* Eau Claire, WI: Thinking Publications.

Crais, E., and Lorch, N. (1994). Oral narratives in school-age children. *Topics in Language Disorders, 14*(3), 13–28.

Flynn, K. (1995). *Graphic organizers: Helping children think visually.* Cypress, CA: Creative Teaching Press.

Glenn, C., and Stein, N. (1980). *Syntactic structures and real-world themes in stories generated by children.* Urbana, IL: University of Illinois, Center for the Study of Reading.

Hedberg, N., and Stoel-Gammon, C. (1986). Narrative analysis: Clinical procedures. *Topics in Language Disorders, 7*(1), 58–69.

Hedberg, N., and Westby, C. (1993). *Analyzing storytelling skills: Theory to practice.* Tucson, AZ: Communication Skill Builders.

Hughes, D., McGillivray, L., and Schmidek, M. (1997). *Guide to narrative language: Procedures for assessment.* Eau Claire, WI: Thinking Publications.

Kemper, S., and Edwards, L. (1986). Children's expression of causality and their construction of narratives. *Topics in Language Disorders, 7*(1), 11–20.

Larson, V., and McKinley, N. (1987). *Communication assessment and intervention strategies for adolescents.* Eau Claire, WI: Thinking Publications.

Larson, V. Lord, and McKinley, N. (1995). *Language disorders in older students: Preadolescents and adolescents.* Eau Claire, WI: Thinking Publications.

Montgomery, J. (1998). *Literacy as a key element of our speech and language interventions.* Paper presented at the American Speech-Language-Hearing Association's Achieving Successful Outcomes in Schools convention, Chicago, IL.

Nelson, N.W. (1993). *Childhood language disorders in context: Infancy through adolescence.* New York: Macmillan.

Narrative Toolbox

Nicolosi, L., Harryman, E., and Kresheck, J. (1996). *Terminology of communication disorders: Speech-language-hearing* (4th ed.). Baltimore: Williams and Wilkins.

Norris, J., and Brunig, R. (1988). Cohesion in the narratives of good and poor readers. *Journal of Speech and Hearing Disorders, 53*(4), 416–424.

Page, J., and Stewart, S. (1985). Story grammar skills in school-age children. *Topics in Language Disorders, 5*(2), 16–30.

Roth, F., and Spekman, N. (1985, June). *Story grammar analysis of narratives produced by learning disabled and normally achieving students.* Paper presented at the Symposium on Research in Child Language Disorders, Madison, WI.

Roth, F., and Spekman, N. (1986). Narrative disclosure: Spontaneously generated stories of learning-disabled and normally achieving students. *Journal of Speech and Hearing Disorders, 51*(1), 8–23.

Scott, C. (1988). A perspective on the evaluation of school children's narratives. *Language, Speech, and Hearing Services in Schools, 19*(1), 67–82.

Silliman, E., and Wilkinson, L. (1991). *Communicating for learning: Classroom observation and collaboration.* Gaithersburg, MD: Aspen.

Stein, N., and Glenn, C. (1979). An analysis of story comprehension in elementary school children. In R. Freedle (Ed.), *New directions in discourse processing* (pp. 53–120). Hillsdale, NJ: Erlbaum.

Strong, C. (1998). *The Strong narrative assessment procedure (SNAP).* Eau Claire, WI: Thinking Publications.

Van Dongen, R., and Westby, C. (1986). Building the narrative mode of thought through children's literature. *Topics in Language Disorders, 7*(1), 70–83.

Vygotsky, L.S. (1962). *Thought and language.* Cambridge, MA: MIT Press.

Westby, C. (1984). Development of narrative language abilities. In G. Wallach and K. Butler (Eds.), *Language learning disabilities in school-age children* (pp. 103–127). Baltimore: Williams and Wilkins.

Westby, C. (1991). *Learning to talk—Talking to learn: Oral-literate language differences.* In C. Simon (Ed.), Communication skills and classroom success (pp. 334–355). Eau Claire, WI: Thinking Publications.